GILBERT VS. SULLIVAN

Book by

STANLEY RALPH ROSS

Music by

SIR ARTHUR SULLIVAN

Lryics by

SIR WILLIAM GILBERT

Dramatic Publishing

Woodstock, Illinois • England • Australia • New Zealand

*** NOTICE ***

ISBN 0-87129-991-7

IMPORTANT BILLING AND CREDIT REQUIREMENTS

All producers of the play *must* give credit to the author(s) of the play in all programs distributed in connection with performances of the play and in all instances in which the title of the play appears for purposes of advertising, publicizing or otherwise exploiting the play and/or a production. The name of the author(s) *must* also appear on a separate line, on which no other name appears, immediately following the title, and *must* appear in size of type not less than fifty percent the size of the title type. Biographical information on the author(s), if included in this book, may be used on all programs. *On all programs this notice must appear:*

"Produced by special arrangement with
THE DRAMATIC PUBLISHING COMPANY of Woodstock, Illinois"

SONGS

ACT ONE

H.M.S. Pinafore

1. "We Sail the Ocean Blue" .... Chorus
2. "I'm Called Little Buttercup"............. Buttercup
3. "I Am the Captain of the Pinafore" .... Captain/Chorus
4. "We Sail the Ocean Blue"/"Gaily Tripping" Crew/Sisters/Cousins/Aunts
5. "The Monarch of the Sea" .... Grossmith/Females

5b. "When I Was a Lad" .... Grossmith

6. "Finale" (from "Carefully on Tiptoe Stealing" to end) All

Pirates Of Penzance

7. "I Am a Pirate King" .... Pirate King/Chorus
8. "Poor Wandering One" .... Mabel/Sisters
9. "I Am the Very Model of a Modern Major-General" Grossmith
10. (Reprise) "I Am the Very Model of a Modern Major-General" .... Major-General/Ensemble
11. "When the Foeman Bares His Steel" .... Men/Women
12. "A Policeman's Lot" .... Sergeant/Police
13. (Finale) "Take Heart" .... All

ACT TWO

Patience

14. "When I First Put This Uniform On" . . . . Colonel/Men
15. "If You're Anxious" . . . . Bunthorne

Iolanthe

16. "The Nightmare Song" . . . . Grossmith
17. "Faint Heart Never Won Fair Lady". . . . . Male trio

The Mikado

18. "If You Want to Know Who We Are" . . . . Chorus
19. "A Wandering Minstrel I". . . . . Nanki-Poo/Chorus
20. "Defer, Defer"/"As Someday It May Happen"
Ko-Ko/Chorus
21. "Three Little Maids" . . . . Female trio/Chorus
22. "Here's a How-Dee-Do" . . . . Mixed trio
23. "Miya Sama"/"A More Humane Mikado"
Mikado/Katisha/Chorus
24. "The Flowers That Bloom in the Spring". . . . . Trio
25. "Titwillow" . . . . Ko-Ko
26. "Finale" (from "For He's Gone and Married Yum-Yum")
All

GILBERT VS. SULLIVAN

A Musical in Two Acts
For 8 men, 4 women, singers, dancers, chorus

CHARACTERS

William S. Gilbert
Arthur Sullivan
Rupert D'oyly Carte
(also plays Rupert D'oyly Carte Jr.)
Rutland Barrington
(also plays Pirate King, Bunthorne, The Mikado)
George Grossmith
(also plays Sir Joseph, Major General, Lord Chancellor)
Feature Player One
(plays The Colonel, Lord Tolloler, Nanki-Poo)
Feature Player Two
(plays Police Sergeant, Lord Mountararat)
Feature Player Three
(plays Oscar Wilde, Koko)
Lucy "Kitten" Gilbert
(also plays Blanche Roosevelt, Yum-Yum)
Fanny Ronalds
(also plays Peep-Bo)
Bridget D'oyly Carte
(also plays Pitti-Sing)
Harriet Everhard
(also plays Buttercup, Cousin Hebe, Katisha)

ACT ONE

("Overture." This music is comprised of tunes from Trial by Jury *and* The Sorcerer. *They are yet to be chosen but a generous selection might include: "The Judge's Song," "Oh, Gentlemen, Listen, I Pray," from the former; and "My Name is John Wellington Welles," "Now to the Banquet We Press," "Country Dance" and "Finale" from the latter.*

AT RISE: *Int. Rupert D'Oyly Carte's living room DR—May 30, 1911. A small set with a large lounging chair, a table and a free-standing lamp. RUPERT D'OYLY CARTE, 36, reads a newspaper while his young daughter, BRIDGET, a teenager, stands nearby. He closes the paper, sighs.*

RUPERT. That's it then. Gilbert's gone. The last of the trio.

BRIDGET. How did he die?

RUPERT. The same way he lived, chasing after a young woman.

BRIDGET. Truly?

RUPERT. Two of his pubescent "proteges" were swimming in three feet of water on his country estate. One thought she was having a cramp so Gilbert, ever the gallant gentleman, dove in to help. The shock was evidently too much for his 75-year-old body.

BRIDGET. I never met any of them. What were they like?

RUPERT. Everything you've ever heard or read about Gilbert and Sullivan and your grandfather was a pack of lies.

BRIDGET. But they *hated* each other ... didn't they?

RUPERT. Not at all. People who hate each other could never have devised such memorable work. They respected each others' talents immensely, they argued like lovers, they battled over the most inane trifles but they were as close as two human beings could be who never kissed.

BRIDGET. And grandfather?

RUPERT. He was their minister, their producer and their referee. We shall not see their likes again. I was too young for *Trial by Jury* or *The Sorcerer* but I recall *H.M.S. Pinafore* and it's as though it were yesterday when I would sneak into their rehearsals. If the Savoy walls could only speak. Better yet, if they could sing.

(Fade down lights at DR, lights full up at center stage. Strike small set. Int. Opera Comique, London, Afternoon, May 4, 1878. The set is the quarterdeck of the H.M.S. Pinafore. SAILORS, led by BOATSWAIN, are discovered cleaning brass work, splitting rope., etc. They are a tatterdemalion lot; some dressed totally in rehearsal clothes of the era, others partially costumed: a hat or a top or naval trousers; none is in full naval regalia. Music begins as curtain rises.)

(MUSIC 1: "WE SAIL THE OCEAN BLUE")

CHORUS.

WE SAIL THE OCEAN BLUE,
AND OUR SAUCY SHIP'S A BEAUTY.
WE'RE SOBER MEN AND TRUE,
AND ATTENTIVE TO OUR DUTY.
WHEN THE BALLS WHISTLE FREE,
O'ER THE BRIGHT, BLUE SEA
WE STAND TO OUR GUNS ALL DAY
WHEN AT ANCHOR WE RIDE
ON THE PORTSMOUTH TIDE,
WE'VE PLENTY OF TIME FOR PLAY.

(LITTLE BUTTERCUP enters, with a large basket on her arm. An older woman [HARRIET EVERHARD] with a face that looks like the inside of a torn pocket. Segue.)

(MUSIC 2: "I'M CALLED LITTLE BUTTERCUP")

BUTTERCUP *(recites).*

HAIL MAN-O-WAR'S MEN—
SAFEGUARDS OF YOUR NATION
HERE IS AN END, AT LAST,
OF ALL PRIVATION,
YOU'VE GOT YOUR PAY—
SPARE ALL YOU CAN AFFORD,
TO WELCOME LITTLE BUTTERCUP ON BOARD.
I'M CALLED LITTLE BUTTERCUP
DEAR LITTLE BUTTERCUP
THOUGH I COULD NEVER TELL WHY
BUT STILL I'M CALLED BUTTERCUP
POOR LITTLE BUTTERCUP
SWEET LITTLE BUTTERCUP, I!

I'VE SNUFF AND TOBACCY, AND EXCELLENT JACKY,
I'VE SCISSORS AND WATCHES AND KNIVES,
I'VE RIBBONS AND LACES TO SET OFF THE FACES,
OF PRETTY YOUNG SWEETHEARTS AND WIVES.

I'VE TREACLE AND TOFFEE,
I'VE TEA AND I'VE COFFEE,
SOFT TOMMY AND SUCCULENT CHOPS,
I'VE CHICKENS AND CONIES
AND PRETTY POLONIES
AND EXCELLENT PEPPERMINT DROPS.

THEN BUY OF YOUR BUTTERCUP
DEAR LITTLE BUTTERCUP,
SAILORS SHOULD NEVER BE SHY.
SO, BUY OF YOUR BUTTERCUP
POOR LITTLE BUTTERCUP
COME, OF YOUR BUTTERCUP, BUY.

(Song ends. Cast awaits, apparently unstaged. Two men stride down the aisle from the rear of theatre. One is tall, imperious, mustached and bearded. He wears a suit, carries a sheaf of papers and is given to bombast. This is WILLIAM S. GILBERT. He talks as though he is a barrister. Which he is. The second man is ARTHUR SEYMOUR SULLIVAN, somewhat smaller, softer of voice and gentler of nature, also bearded in the nature of the era's style. Both are impeccably dressed and will add avoirdupois *during the evening as they age.)*

SULLIVAN *(walking toward stage)*. Absolutely marvelous!

GILBERT *(walking toward stage)*. Positively terrible!

SULLIVAN. Well, the third tenor *was* a quarter tone off on his fourth line, but ...

GILBERT. My dear Sullivan, you know full well that my musical ear is miles closer to *tin* than flesh. Only a rash man ever asked me to hum, but that situation was desperate. However, I *do* think the third tenor has splendid diction, and that, after all, is what matters, isn't it?

SULLIVAN. Well, they *are* singing music, you know, and—

GILBERT. They surely are, and what magnificent music it is. However, a song without words is not a song at all. It doesn't matter if one is singing French or Italian or even German opera. No decent Englishman understands what they're saying anyhow.

SULLIVAN. And yet ...

GILBERT *(as he climbs stage)*. So! We are agreed then! Let clarity of speech be our main consideration.

SULLIVAN *(climbs stage)*. I believe this is something that should *not* be discussed before a cast.

(The cast watches as the two approach each other at center stage.)

GILBERT. Nonsense! This concerns them as well. *(Nods to cast, they nod back.)*

SULLIVAN. Very well, then, if you want to have it out right here, let's have it out right here!

(RICHARD D'OYLY CARTE enters. A small, tight man, exquisitely dressed. Oil on troubled waters. [The same actor who plays RUPERT].)

CARTE. Just a moment! Before this dispute erupts into a brouhaha, may I suggest you meet halfway?

SULLIVAN *(stiffens)*. Any man willing to meet you half way is usually a poor judge of distance.

CARTE. Well, can't we work out a compromise?

GILBERT *(equally stiff)*. A compromise is an agreement by which *either* side gets what *neither* side wanted! Now you can do us *both* a favor...

SULLIVAN *(finishes sentence)*. ...by paying attention to financial matters only and leaving the creativity to us, *Mr.* Carte!

GILBERT. Well put, my dear Sullivan.

SULLIVAN. Thank you, my dear Gilbert.

(They shake hands. CARTE shakes his head. You can't win. The soprano portraying BUTTERCUP ahems.)

GILBERT. What *is* it, Harriet?

HARRIET. I should like to *move* more.

GILBERT. Move as much as you care to, Harriet, but *not* while you're on *our* stage singing *our* songs.

HARRIET. I feel rooted to the spot. Why must I stand in one place? After all, I'm *not* a chorus girl.

GILBERT. No, madam, your voice is not strong enough or, no doubt, you *would* be!

(She walks off in a snit.)

CARTE. Do you mind if I say something?

GILBERT & SULLIVAN *(as one)*. Yes!

CARTE. It has nothing to do with the songs or the libretto.

SULLIVAN. Then say it, Carte, and don't shilly shally! We open in two weeks and this show is an absolute shambles.

CARTE. Well, it's a money matter and since we share expenses as well as profits, you *should* be made aware of it.

GILBERT. You're not going to dredge up that old bellyache about spending too much on the costumes, are you?

(No answer from CARTE. Of course, that's exactly what he was about to mention.)

GILBERT. *Are* you?

CARTE. Uhm... We can talk about it later. *(Walks toward cast.)*

GILBERT *(to SULLIVAN)*. He's outraged because I've had the sailor suits designed and made by a naval tailor down at Portsmouth.

CARTE. They could have been done for half-price by any local seamstress.

GILBERT. Yes, but if these men are to *portray* sailors, they must *feel* like sailors. Everything must be done with total authenticity and sincerity. *(To the cast.)* And may I remind you all that the moment you *think* you're funny, the audience ceases to laugh! Now, let's go over the lines. The problem is that we are our own worst rivals and each new work makes our task more difficult.

(GILBERT walks upstage and gathers the men around him as SULLIVAN and CARTE walk DR. In background, the actors softly repeat the lyrics of the opening number, not loud enough to disturb the dialogue in foreground.)

CARTE *(sighs, shakes his head)*. An impossible man.

SULLIVAN *(sighs)*. Yes, but he is a genius and they are in quite short supply these days.

CARTE. You've written a marvelous score, Arthur.

SULLIVAN. Do you really think so?

CARTE. Your best yet.

SULLIVAN. To me, all of the songs just seem to serve Gilbert's clever lyrics, nothing more. I'd love the opportunity to write some *good* music. I went to the Royal Academy where I was a Mendelssohn scholar.

CARTE. You've already written any number of important pieces.

SULLIVAN. Yes ... yes ... but the truth is I'm only doing *this* for the money.

CARTE. Well, aren't we all? It's what supports our life-style.

(GILBERT is finished with the men, comes downstage, shouts.)

GILBERT. Barrington! Front and center!

(A man wearing a captain's hat and a heavily braided coat enters. This is RUTLAND BARRINGTON.)

BARRINGTON. Yes, Mr. Gilbert?

(CARTE walks to BARRINGTON, runs his hands along the braiding.)

CARTE. Now this is *exactly* what I'm annoyed about. The three of us are paying for all this folderol. It's an excessive expense and certainly *not* important to the production. *(Rips the braiding off one arm of the astonished BARRINGTON.)*

GILBERT. Why don't we do the job properly? *(Rips braiding off other arm.)* And what about the hat? *(Takes hat off BARRINGTON's head, puts it on floor, jumps on it.)*

CARTE. Gilbert, there's no need to...

GILBERT. Are you happy now, Mr. *Oily* Carte? This outfit, replete with all the braid, is *precisely* what real captains wear! Now, if you've finished destroying our rehearsals, we would like to continue in an orderly fashion.

(CARTE stares at GILBERT, whirls and walks off. At CARTE's exit, GILBERT's mood is jolly once more, turns to BARRINGTON.)

GILBERT. Do you know your words, Barrington?

BARRINGTON. Absolutely, sir. The music, too.

SULLIVAN. Thank you.

BARRINGTON. And thank *you* both for giving me such a wonderful role. I'd have thought you'd require a handsome man with a large voice.

GILBERT *(arm around BARRINGTON's shoulder)*. That's precisely what we *don't* want. Singers with large voices usually have egos to match. *Your* ego is the same size as your vocal chords. Tiny and perfect!

SULLIVAN. We prefer using performers without previous experience. That way, they have no exaggerated sense of themselves.

GILBERT. Further, they have nothing to *un*learn. Now, let's get to it!

(MUSIC 3: "I AM THE CAPTAIN OF THE PINAFORE")

CAPTAIN.
MY GALLANT CREW, GOOD MORNING.

CHORUS *(saluting)*.
SIR! GOOD MORNING!

CAPTAIN.
I HOPE YOU'RE ALL QUITE WELL.

CHORUS.
QUITE WELL, AND YOU, SIR?

CAPTAIN.
I AM IN REASONABLE HEALTH,
AND HAPPY TO MEET YOU ALL ONCE MORE.

CHORUS.
YOU DO US PROUD, SIR!

CAPTAIN.
I AM THE CAPTAIN OF THE PINAFORE,

CHORUS.
AND A RIGHT GOOD CAPTAIN, TOO!

CAPTAIN.
YOU'RE VERY VERY GOOD,
AND BE IT UNDERSTOOD,
I COMMAND A RIGHT GOOD CREW.

CHORUS.

WE'RE VERY VERY GOOD,
AND BE IT UNDERSTOOD,
HE COMMANDS A RIGHT GOOD CREW.

CAPTAIN.

THOUGH RELATED TO A PEER,
I CAN HAND, REEF AND STEER
OR SHIP A SELVAGEE
I AM NEVER KNOWN TO QUAIL
AT THE FURY OF A GALE
AND I'M NEVER NEVER SICK AT SEA.

CHORUS.

WHAT, NEVER?

CAPTAIN.

NO, NEVER!

CHORUS.

WHAT, *NEVER*?

CAPTAIN.

HARDLY EVER!

CHORUS.

HE'S HARDLY EVER SICK AT SEA!
THEN GIVE THREE CHEERS
AND ONE CHEER MORE
FOR THE HARDY CAPTAIN OF THE PINAFORE.
THEN GIVE THREE CHEERS
AND ONE CHEER MORE FOR...
THE CAPTAIN OF THE PINAFORE.

CAPTAIN.

I DO MY BEST TO SATISFY YOU ALL

CHORUS.

AND WITH YOU WE'RE QUITE CONTENT.

CAPTAIN.

YOU'RE EXCEEDINGLY POLITE,
AND I THINK IT ONLY RIGHT
TO RETURN THE COMPLIMENT!

CHORUS.

WE'RE EXCEEDINGLY POLITE,
AND HE THINKS IT'S ONLY RIGHT
TO RETURN THE COMPLIMENT!

CAPTAIN.

BAD LANGUAGE OR ABUSE,
I NEVER, NEVER USE
WHATEVER THE EMERGENCY,
THOUGH "BOTHER IT" I MAY
OCCASIONALLY SAY,
I NEVER USE A BIG, BIG "D"

CHORUS.

WHAT, NEVER?

CAPTAIN.

NO, NEVER.

CHORUS.

WHAT, NEVER?

CAPTAIN.

HARDLY EVER...

CHORUS.

HARDLY EVER SWEARS A BIG, BIG "D"—
THEN GIVE THREE CHEERS
AND ONE CHEER MORE
FOR THE WELL-BRED CAPTAIN OF THE PINAFORE.
THEN GIVE THREE CHEERS
AND ONE CHEER MORE
FOR...THE CAPTAIN OF THE PINAFORE.

(Song ends. GILBERT and SULLIVAN approach BARRINGTON from either side, pump his hand in congratulations.)

GILBERT. Excellent, I understood every word.

SULLIVAN. And I recognized every note.

GILBERT. What more could we ask? Keep up the impressive work and, please, what*ever* you do, *don't* take any singing lessons! Off with you now.

(BARRINGTON exits. GILBERT turns and shouts offstage.)

GILBERT. Grossmith!!!

(GEORGE GROSSMITH, reed-thin nervous, skin stretched over anxiety, enters. He wears an outlandish naval costume, quite overdone, with a large plumed hat. SULLIVAN examines the costume, amused.)

SULLIVAN. 'Tis a bit *much*, isn't it? Carte would have a stroke.

GILBERT. *Au contraire*, my dear fellow. It's an exact duplicate of what the first sea lord wears with just a little *less* gold braid. On matters such as this, kindly trust me. *(To GROSSMITH.)* Are you prepared, George?

GROSSMITH. Yes, Mr. Gilbert.

GILBERT. While onstage, you must never lose sight of the fact that you are satirizing W.H. Smith, the first sea lord, news agent to millions and a sailor who *never* went to sea.

SULLIVAN *(aside)*. That statement, George, is strictly between us, and we are prepared to deny it in every court in the land.

(From here, GILBERT and SULLIVAN are having the jumpy little actor on, and he never realizes it.)

GILBERT. Comedy is a serious business, George, and there *may* be murder threats from various steadfast members of the armed forces who will be far from gruntled by your comic portrayal of their hero.

GROSSMITH. But ... but ... I don't know how Smith *speaks* or even how he *looks* so how can I possibly avoid any similarities?

SULLIVAN *(rubs his chin as he mulls that)*. Hmm, in that case, just do it the way Gilbert taught you and, for the sake of your survivors, I'd make certain your last will and testament is in order and your life insurance is paid up to date.

GROSSMITH *(really frightened)*. But ... you mean ... death threats? Oh, my!

SULLIVAN. If you would prefer to step aside and let your understudy have the role, there would be no hard feelings.

(An UNDERSTUDY [part of the CHORUS] steps forward. GILBERT puts the hat on the youth's head.)

GILBERT. Yes, you could always go back to being a crime reporter at Bow Street Police Station or whatever it was you did before we plucked you out of obscurity.

(GROSSMITH grabs the hat off the youth's head, rises to his full short height. Disappointed, the UNDERSTUDY returns to the CHORUS.)

GROSSMITH. I will *never* be intimidated by anyone!
GILBERT. What, never?
SULLIVAN. Well, hardly ever!

(They all laugh.)

GILBERT. Get on with it, George.

(GROSSMITH exits. Music begins.)

(MUSIC 4: "WE SAIL THE OCEAN BLUE"/ "GAILY TRIPPING")

FEMALES.
GAILY TRIPPING, LIGHTLY SKIPPING
FLOCK THE MAIDENS TO THE SHIPPING.

GAILY TRIPPING, LIGHTLY SKIPPING
FLOCK THE MAIDENS TO THE SHIPPING

SAILORS.

FLAGS AND GUNS AND PENNANTS DIPPING
ALL THE LADIES LOVE THE SHIPPING.

FEMALES.

SAILORS SPRIGHTLY,
ALWAYS RIGHTLY,
WELCOME LADIES SO POLITELY.

SAILORS.

LADIES WHO CAN SMILE SO BRIGHTLY,
SAILORS WELCOME MOST POLITELY
WELCOME MOST POLITELY

FEMALES.

SAILORS SPRIGHTLY
ALWAYS RIGHTLY,
WELCOME LADIES SO POLITELY.

(Sung simultaneously.)

FEMALES & BASSES	TENOR SAILORS
GAILY TRIPPING, LIGHTLY SKIPPING,	**WE'RE SMART AND SOBER MEN**
FLOCK THE MAIDENS TO THE SHIPPING,	**AND QUITE DEVOID OF FEAR**
GAILY TRIPPING, LIGHTLY SKIPPING,	**IN ALL THE ROYAL N.**
FLOCK THE MAIDENS TO THE SHIPPING.	**NONE ARE SO SMART AS WE ARE**

(Sung simultaneously.)

FEMALES	SAILORS
SAILORS SPRIGHTLY, ALWAYS RIGHTLY,	**LADIES WHO CAN SMILE SO BRIGHTLY,**
WELCOME LADIES SO POLITELY,	**SAILORS WELCOME MOST POLITELY**
SO POLITELY,	**SO POLITELY,**
GAILY TRIPPING,	**GAILY TRIPPING,**
LIGHTLY SKIPPING,	**LIGHTLY SKIPPING,**
SAILORS ALWAYS	**SAILORS ALWAYS**
WELCOME LADIES MOST POLITELY.	**WELCOME LADIES MOST POLITELY.**

(MUSIC 5: "THE MONARCH OF THE SEA")

(SIR JOSEPH [GROSSMITH] and COUSIN HEBE [female] enter.)

CAPTAIN *(from the poop deck).*
NOW GIVE THREE CHEERS.
I'LL LEAD THE WAY!

CHORUS.
HURRAH! HURRAH! HURRAH! HURRAY!

SIR JOSEPH.
I AM THE MONARCH OF THE SEA,
THE RULER OF THE QUEEN'S NAVEE,
WHOSE PRAISE GREAT BRITAIN LOUDLY CHANTS,

COUSIN HEBE.

AND WE ARE HIS SISTERS AND HIS COUSINS AND HIS AUNTS!

FEMALE RELATIVES.

AND WE ARE HIS SISTERS AND HIS COUSINS AND HIS AUNTS!

ALL.

HIS SISTERS AND HIS COUSINS AND HIS AUNTS!

SIR JOSEPH.

WHEN AT ANCHOR HERE I RIDE,
MY BOSOM SWELLS WITH PRIDE.
AND I SNAP MY FINGERS AT A FOEMAN'S TAUNTS,

COUSIN HEBE.

AND SO DO HIS SISTERS AND HIS COUSINS AND HIS AUNTS!

RELATIVES.

AND SO DO HIS SISTERS AND HIS COUSINS AND HIS AUNTS!

ALL.

HIS SISTERS AND HIS COUSINS AND HIS AUNTS!

SIR JOSEPH.

BUT WHEN THE BREEZES BLOW,
I GENERALLY GO BELOW,
AND SEEK THE SECLUSION THAT A CABIN GRANTS!

COUSIN HEBE.

AND SO DO HIS SISTERS AND HIS COUSINS AND HIS AUNTS!

FEMALE RELATIVES.

AND SO DO HIS SISTERS AND HIS COUSINS AND HIS AUNTS.

ALL.

AND SO DO HIS SISTERS AND HIS COUSINS AND HIS AUNTS
HIS SISTERS AND HIS COUSINS AND HIS AUNTS
WHOM HE RECKONS UP BY DOZENS, AND HIS AUNTS!

(MUSIC 5B: "WHEN I WAS A LAD")

SIR JOSEPH.

WHEN I WAS A LAD I SERVED A TERM AS OFFICE BOY TO AN ATTORNEY'S FIRM,
I CLEANED THE WINDOWS AND I SWEPT THE FLOOR,
AND I POLISHED UP THE HANDLE OF THE BIG FRONT DOOR.

CHORUS.

HE POLISHED UP THE HANDLE OF THE BIG FRONT DOOR.

SIR JOSEPH.

I POLISHED UP THAT HANDLE SO CAREFULLEE,
THAT NOW I AM THE RULER OF THE QUEEN'S NAVEE.

CHORUS.

HE POLISHED UP THAT HANDLE SO CAREFULLEE,
THAT NOW HE IS THE RULER OF THE QUEEN'S NAVEE.

SIR JOSEPH.

AS OFFICE BOY I MADE SUCH A MARK
THAT THEY GAVE ME THE POST OF A JUNIOR CLERK,
I SERVED THE WRITS WITH A SMILE SO BLAND,
AND I COPIED ALL THE LETTERS IN A BIG ROUND HAND.

CHORUS.

HE COPIED ALL THE LETTERS IN A BIG ROUND HAND.

SIR JOSEPH.

I COPIED ALL THE LETTERS IN A HAND SO FREE, THAT NOW I AM THE RULER OF THE QUEEN'S NAVEE

CHORUS.

HE COPIED ALL THE LETTERS IN A HAND SO FREE,
THAT NOW HE IS THE RULER OF THE QUEEN'S NAVEE.

SIR JOSEPH.

IN SERVING WRITS I MADE SUCH A NAME,
THAT AN ARTICLED CLERK I SOON BECAME,

I WORE CLEAN COLLARS AND A BRAND NEW SUIT,
FOR THE PASS EXAMINATION AT THE INSTITUTE.

CHORUS.
FOR THE PASS EXAMINATION AT THE INSTITUTE.

SIR JOSEPH.
THAT PASS EXAMINATION DID SO WELL FOR ME,
THAT NOW I AM THE RULER OF THE QUEEN'S NAVEE.

CHORUS.
THAT PASS EXAMINATION DID SO WELL FOR HE
THAT NOW HE IS THE RULER OF THE QUEEN'S NAVEE.

SIR JOSEPH.
OF LEGAL KNOWLEDGE I ACQUIRED SUCH A GRIP
THAT THEY TOOK ME INTO THE PARTNERSHIP.
AND THAT JUNIOR PARTNERSHIP I WEEN,
WAS THE ONLY SHIP THAT I EVER HAD SEEN.

CHORUS.
WAS THE ONLY SHIP HE EVER HAD SEEN.

SIR JOSEPH.
BUT THAT KIND OF SHIP SO SUITED ME

THAT NOW I AM THE RULER OF THE QUEEN'S NAVEE.

CHORUS.

BUT THAT KIND OF SHIP SO SUITED HE
THAT NOW HE IS THE RULER OF THE QUEEN'S NAVEE.

SIR JOSEPH.

I GREW SO RICH THAT I WAS SENT
BY A POCKET BOROUGH INTO PARLIAMENT.
I ALWAYS VOTED AT MY PARTY'S CALL,
AND I NEVER THOUGHT OF THINKING FOR MYSELF AT ALL.

CHORUS.

HE NEVER THOUGHT OF THINKING FOR HIMSELF AT ALL.

SIR JOSEPH.

I THOUGHT SO LITTLE, THEY REWARDED ME,
BY MAKING ME THE RULER OF THE QUEEN'S NAVEE.

CHORUS.

HE THOUGHT SO LITTLE, THEY REWARDED HE,
BY MAKING HIM THE RULER OF THE QUEEN'S NAVEE.

SIR JOSEPH.

NOW LANDSMEN ALL WHO EVER YOU MAY BE,
IF YOU WANT TO RISE TO THE TOP OF THE TREE,

YOUR SOUL ISN'T FETTERED TO AN OFFICE STOOL,
BE CAREFUL TO BE GUIDED BY THIS GOLDEN RULE.

CHORUS.
BE CAREFUL TO BE GUIDED BY THIS GOLDEN RULE.

SIR JOSEPH.
STICK CLOSE TO YOUR DESKS, AND NEVER GO TO SEA
AND YOU ALL MAY BE RULERS OF THE QUEEN'S NAVEE.

CHORUS.
STICK CLOSE TO YOUR DESKS AND NEVER GO TO SEA,
AND YOU ALL MAY BE THE RULERS OF THE QUEEN'S NAVEE.

(Song ends. Actors move to various places onstage as GILBERT and SULLIVAN flank GROSSMITH [SIR JOSEPH], who waits for a reaction.)

SULLIVAN. Quite good, actually, but when you sing "Now Landsmen All," don't hold the note too long. It's a fine note, George, one of your best, perhaps, but kindly do *not* confuse *your* voice with *my* composition.

GILBERT. Sullivan's music is, as it always is, most melodious, and I heard every note with pristine purity, but there were one or two words in the third stanza which you swallowed like a lion attacking a bunny. Therefore,

I would sincerely appreciate it if... *(He sees his wife in the wings.)*

(LUCY [KITTEN] GILBERT, very attractive, slim, well-turned-out, enters. GILBERT's attitude softens immediately. He adores her.)

GILBERT. Hello, darling.

KITTEN. Please don't stop on my account. *(With affection.)* Next to you, I enjoy hearing you speak more than anyone.

GILBERT. Let me get you a seat. *(Shouts.)* Someone get my wife a seat!

(Four actors race on carrying chairs.)

KITTEN. One will be sufficient, thank you. *(To SULLIVAN.)* Hello, Arthur. You look well.

SULLIVAN. Looks are deceiving.

GILBERT. Have you had your tea yet?

KITTEN. No, but I didn't want to disturb anything and...

GILBERT. Let me get you some tea. *(Shouts.)* Somebody get my wife some tea! Better yet, let's *all* have tea. *(To the cast.)* We should learn a lesson from tea, ladies and gentlemen. Its real strength emerges when it's in hot water.

(GILBERT takes his wife by the hand, and they repair to an area DL, where a few actors have tea and biscuits. SULLIVAN moves DR to the footlights. CARTE enters from the audience.)

CARTE. I heard what you said. Are you still in pain?

SULLIVAN. You don't know what pain is until you pass a kidney stone. It's like trying to cram a bowling ball into a drinking straw. I've not been myself since my brother, Fred, died.

CARTE *(nods)*. A great tragedy for the musical theatre. How is your mother taking it?

SULLIVAN. Poorly. Now I'm all she has so I spend every waking moment with her. Add that to the task of facing Gilbert daily and you can imagine my general mood. Music is a brutal mistress. As soon as we open, I'm off to Monte Carlo for some sunshine and roulette without my other mistress.

CARTE. You're not taking Mrs. Ronalds with you?

SULLIVAN. Would that I could, but she's still married and society's eyebrows would rise to new heights.

CARTE. She hasn't lived with him for years. Why not arrive a few days apart and announce that you are only good friends?

SULLIVAN *(laughs)*. Ah, yes... "Good friends." The genteel euphemism for two people who sleep together... in separate rooms. Everyone who is anyone will be at Monte Carlo and their mouths will continue to work long after their consciences have ceased to function.

(GILBERT walks forward, claps his hands.)

GILBERT. Places, everyone. Tea break is over. Time, as our pecuniary partner continues to remind us, is money. Act two, song six. Everyone on stage, we'll do the finale.

BARRINGTON. I haven't finished my tea yet.

GILBERT. Sorry, Barrington. You may certainly finish your tea. Would you prefer doing it in someone else's show?

(BARRINGTON gulps the tea down, falls into place next to the others, tosses the cup and saucer to another actor. GILBERT pulls a chair over and indicates KITTEN sit in it.)

KITTEN. Oh, Winkie, you're so forceful.

GILBERT *(to others)*. Will you excuse me for just a moment? *(GILBERT walks to MRS. GILBERT, takes her aside, speaks sotto voce.)* My sweet, I must caution you to *never* use that name when we are in public. Winkie is something one calls *his* dog, not *her* husband.

KITTEN. What do you call Arthur?

GILBERT. Sullivan and I have never referred to each other by anything but our surnames, nor do we intend to. It's the gentlemanly thing to do.

KITTEN. That is carrying gentlemanlyness to preposterous lengths. This is the fourth show you've written together. By this time, being on a first-name basis *might* be forgiven.

GILBERT. It's not us.

KITTEN. I don't understand it. Neither of you are from noble backgrounds. *His* father was a bandmaster and *yours* was a family physician.

GILBERT. Yes, well, to be *born* a gentleman is merely an accident of birth; to die one is an *achievement*.

(CARTE walks forward, joins MR. and MRS. GILBERT.)

CARTE *(looks at his pocket watch)*. Can we continue? The cast goes on overtime in eight minutes.

GILBERT. You're quite right, Carte, quite right. *(Takes KITTEN's arm.)* I'll be home within an hour, my darling. Please have dinner, some red wine and, unless my pet goose has died, six quill pens waiting at my elbow. These lyrics are a muddle.

KITTEN *(waves to everyone)*. Goodbye. Good luck.

GILBERT. One *never* says good luck in the theatre, my darling. It ranks somewhere behind whistling in the dressing room and just ahead of courting the evil eye.

KITTEN. Sorry. What *should* I say? Break a leg?

(In background upstage, a CHORUS member slips and does a pratfall.)

GILBERT. Hmm. Yes, that will do. Break a leg, I must remember that.

(The GILBERTS exit. CARTE sidles to SULLIVAN.)

CARTE. It is quite the most bizarre collaboration I've ever seen. Sort of like Attila the Hun and St. Francis of Assisi.

SULLIVAN. I'm *hardly* St. Francis. *(Beat.)* In truth, there's no one like him. Do you know what he said when we first met?

CARTE. I couldn't possibly imagine.

SULLIVAN *(reaches into his pocket, removes paper)*. Well, he freely admits he is ignorant about music. He claims he can recognize just two songs. One is "God Save the Queen"...

CARTE. And the other one ... isn't. Yes, I know.

SULLIVAN. The first time we met, and I've written it down because it's so wonderfully silly, he said ... *(Reads.)* "Pleased to meet you, Mr. Sullivan, because you're able to settle a question which has been bothering me. My contention is that when a musician has a theme to express, he can do it perfectly upon the simple tetrachord of Mercury, in which there are, no diatonic intervals whatsoever, as upon the more elaborate disdiapason—with the familiar four tetrachords and the redundant note, which, I need not remind you, embraces all the single, double and inverted chords."

(SULLIVAN has been laughing and now CARTE is equally convulsed.)

CARTE. What was your answer?

SULLIVAN. After nearly thirty years of musical training, I had *no* idea what he was talking about. He'd stolen all the phrases from the encyclopedia, arranged them in some diabolical order and memorized it specifically for our meeting.

CARTE. Anyone who goes to all that trouble is a valuable friend to have.

SULLIVAN. And yet, we've never *been* friends. Collaborators, yes, but I wonder if we'll ever be able to call each other friends. Still, how could I not appreciate a partner whose foe is folly and whose weapon is wit?

(GILBERT enters, blows a bobby's whistle with a screech.)

GILBERT. Do you like that, Sullivan? I just bought it from a vendor outside.

SULLIVAN. No, I don't like it at all.

GILBERT *(not listening)*. I knew you would, so I bought you one as well. *(He hands whistle to befuddled SULLIVAN, who shakes his head as if to say... "What do you do with a man like that?")* We have three minutes for the finale. Places...

(Actors race to their places.)

GILBERT. We shall rehearse every single song every day until we are flawless. Remember, there's only one person who can always count on steady work in the theatre: the night watchman! Begin!

(Cast moves into place, GILBERT, SULLIVAN, CARTE, step aside.)

(MUSIC 6: "FINALE")

ENSEMBLE.

CAREFULLY ON TIPTOE STEALING,
BREATHING GENTLY AS WE MAY,
EVERY STEP WITH CAUTION FEELING,
WE WILL SOFTLY STEAL AWAY.

(CAPTAIN stamps his foot. Chord!)

ALL.

GOODNESS ME!
WHY, WHAT WAS THAT?

DICK DEAD EYE.

SILENT BE
IT WAS THE CAT!

ALL.

IT WAS!
IT WAS THE CAT!

CAPTAIN *(producing cat-o-nine tails).*

THEY'RE RIGHT!
IT WAS THE CAT!

ALL.

PULL ASHORE, IN FASHION STEADY,
HYMEN WILL DEFRAY THE FARE,
FOR A CLERGYMAN IS READY,
TO UNITE THE HAPPY PAIR.

(CAPTAIN stamps his foot as before. Chord!)

ALL.

GOODNESS ME!
WHY, WHAT WAS THAT?

DICK DEAD EYE.

SILENT BE, AGAIN THE CAT!

ALL.

IT WAS AGAIN THAT CAT!

CAPTAIN *(aside).*

THEY'RE RIGHT, IT WAS THE CAT!
(Throws off his cloak.) **HOLD!**

PRETTY DAUGHTER OF MINE,
I INSIST UPON KNOWING
WHERE YOU MAY BE GOING.
WITH THESE SONS OF THE BRINE.
FOR MY EXCELLENT CREW
THOUGH FOES THEY COULD THUMP ANY,
ARE SCARCELY FIT COMPANY,
MY DAUGHTER, FOR YOU!

CHORUS.
NOW HARK AT THAT, DO!

CREW.
THOUGH FOES WE COULD THUMP ANY,
WE'RE SCARCELY FIT COMPANY
FOR A LADY LIKE YOU!

RALPH RACKSTRAW.
PROUD OFFICER, THAT HAUGHTY LIP UNCURL,
VAIN MAN, SUPPRESS THAT SUPERCILIOUS SNEER,
FOR I HAVE DARED TO LOVE YOUR MATCHLESS GIRL,
A FACT WELL KNOWN TO ALL MY MESSMATES HERE!

CAPTAIN.
OH HORRORS!

RALPH RACKSTRAW & JOSEPHINE.
I *(HE)* HUMBLE, POOR AND LOWLY BORN
THE MEANEST IN THE PORT DIVISION,
THE BUTT OF EPAULETTED SCORN,
THE MARK OF QUARTER-DECK DERISION,

HAVE *(HAS)* DARED TO RAISE *(MY)* HIS WORMY EYES
ABOVE THE DUST TO WHICH YOU'D MOULD *(ME)* HIM,
IN MANHOOD'S GLORIOUS PRIDE TO RISE
I AM *(HE IS)* AN ENGLISHMAN, BEHOLD *(ME)* HIM.

(All cast on stage carrying small British flags.)

ALL.

HE IS AN ENGLISHMAN!

CAPTAIN.

HE IS AN ENGLISHMAN,
FOR HE HIMSELF HAS SAID IT.
AND IT'S GREATLY TO HIS CREDIT
THAT HE IS AN ENGLISHMAN!

ALL.

THAT HE IS AN ENGLISHMAN!

CAPTAIN.

FOR HE MIGHT HAVE BEEN A ROOSIAN,
A FRENCH, A TURK, OR A PROOSIAN,
OR PERHAPS ITALI-AN!

ALL.

OR PERHAPS ITALI-AN!

CAPTAIN.

BUT IN SPITE OF ALL TEMPTATIONS,

TO BELONG TO OTHER NATIONS,
HE REMAINS AN ENGLISHMAN!

ALL.

FOR IN SPITE OF ALL TEMPTATIONS
TO BELONG TO OTHER NATIONS,
HE REMAINS AN ENGLISHMAN!
HE REMAINS AN ENGLISHMAN!

(Song ends. Go to black. Set revolves under cover of darkness to ... Music 6A: Piano Cue. Int. Opera Comique, London—May 10, 1879—afternoon. Assorted flats in background. Piano is at L. Single gas work light for illumination. SULLIVAN sits at the spinet and noodles some melodies. [If the actor can really play, so much the better.] Standing behind him and kneading his shoulders is MRS. FANNY RONALDS, a comely American woman ten years older than SULLIVAN, physically affectionate and psychologically supportive.)

SULLIVAN *(as he rubs his cheek against her arm)*. You have the face of an angel, a body by Michelangelo, and the hands of a saint.

FANNY *(laughs)*. And Gilbert is supposed to have the way with words. *(Beat.)* Play that again, Arthur, The Buttercup Song. It's so catchy.

(He tinkles the tune in background.)

SULLIVAN. Isn't it odd that the music to *Pinafore*, which everyone thought was so happy, was written while I was suffering from my kidney problems?

FANNY. I know.

SULLIVAN. I'd compose a few bars, then almost faint from the pain. After it passed, I'd write a bit more until the pain began again. I wish you could have been with me the entire time.

FANNY. You're aware of the difficulty, Arthur. My husband doesn't care what I do, as long as I'm discreet.

SULLIVAN. Yes, however...

FANNY. And to be seen too often with England's most popular composer is to start tongues wagging. Of every five people who talk about us, four will say something bad and the fifth will say something good... in a bad way.

(SULLIVAN shifts in his chair, and winces appreciably.)

FANNY. You must take something for that pain, Arthur.

SULLIVAN. Medicine is the number one killer of Englishmen. I feel about physicians the way Voltaire did. He said: "Doctors are men who prescribe medicines of which they know little, to cure diseases of which they know less, in human beings of whom they know nothing."

FANNY. He also said: "Their art consists of amusing the patient while God heals the disease."

SULLIVAN. And yet, I've never *met* an amusing doctor. They all seem to have been weaned on a pickle. *(Beat.)* I could accept my pain if you were by my side.

FANNY. He'll never divorce me, Arthur. And why should he? By staying married, he wears the cloak of respectability in the United States, I get enormous support payments and we have each other.

SULLIVAN. But I want you so much to be my wife.

FANNY. It would be wonderful but I think my family might have a problem accepting an Irish-Italian-Jewish son-in-law, no matter *how* famous he is. It's better this way.

(D'OYLY CARTE enters.)

CARTE. Morning, Arthur, morning Mrs. Ronalds. What an ungodly hour! A theatre should never be entered in sunlight, except on matinee days.
SULLIVAN. *You* called the meeting.
CARTE. Yes, well, I would have preferred it at Gilbert's but he insisted on having it here. His place is being renovated, and the noise drives him madder than usual. Have you seen the house yet?
SULLIVAN. Yes. I imagine that's the way the *Queen* would like to live ... if she had Gilbert's money.

(GILBERT enters.)

GILBERT *(cheerily)*. Good morning, Mrs. Ronalds, Sullivan, Carte. I trust you are all well.
FANNY. Nice to see you, William. *(Beat.)* I must be going.
GILBERT. Good Lord! Was it something I said?
FANNY *(laughs)*. Dear me, no. I have a luncheon appointment. Goodbye then, gentlemen.

(FANNY gives SULLIVAN a peck on the cheek, shakes hands with CARTE and GILBERT, exits. GILBERT reaches into his pocket, removes a newspaper cutting.)

CARTE. We must decide where to open the new show.
SULLIVAN. Aren't we doing it here?

GILBERT. Before you answer that, Carte, may I read from *The New York Sun* newspaper, dated three weeks ago yesterday. And I quote: "There are now 98 pirated versions of *H.M.S. Pinafore* playing to packed houses in the United States. Companies formed after 8 p.m. yesterday are not included." The worst of it is that they are probably rotten performers.

SULLIVAN. The U.S. courts seem to feel that an American citizen should not be deprived of his rights of robbing someone else. What can we do?

CARTE. Well, that's why I called this—

GILBERT *(overriding CARTE)*. Perhaps, someday, American jurisprudence will offer the same protection to creators of music and lyrics as they do for the man who invents a better mousetrap!

(Long beat, SULLIVAN and GILBERT turn to CARTE.)

SULLIVAN. What is it you wish to say, Carte?

GILBERT. Don't stand there like a mute. Out with it!

CARTE. I suggest we open the new show in New York. That way, we can copyright it there immediately. Simultaneously, we'll have one of the *Pinafore* touring companies do it here at Paignton, near Portsmouth, and we'll be protected in both countries.

GILBERT. Superb.

SULLIVAN. Appalling. New York is Sodom by the sea. An unfinished mining camp. They'd *never* understand our kind of work.

GILBERT. Ninety-eight pirated versions of Pinafore, none of which is bringing us one brass farthing? I think they understand us only too well.

SULLIVAN. I don't think I'm up to it. My kidneys have been ...

GILBERT. Nonsense, my dear friend. A sea voyage is just the ticket for whatever ails you. Good salt air. Brisk walks around the deck. Much healthier than those smoky gambling dens you frequent.

SULLIVAN. Well ...

GILBERT. Good! It's settled then. *(To CARTE.)* Book us two first-class tickets, Carte, and make sure the ship has a good wine list. *(Looks at wristwatch.)* Must be off now. Nice seeing you both. *(Starts to exit.)*

CARTE. There *is* one other thing. The plot.

GILBERT. What about ... the plot?

CARTE. Well, they *are* rather similar. Except for the fact that one takes place at sea and the other on land. Even the characters seem alike. The critics will murder us.

GILBERT. Authors are no more responsible for their critics than dogs are for their fleas! I *like* the plot and, furthermore, I intend writing the *same* plot until I'm too weak to hold a pen. It's quite basic, actually ... a set of appealing protagonists struggle against seemingly insurmountable odds in quest of a worthwhile goal.

CARTE. But the young lovers, the comic relief, the heinous villains ...

GILBERT *(finishing the sentence)*. ... have all been around since the Greeks. And that time-honored tradition will continue long after all of us have turned to dust. The formula works because that is what people want to see! And that, my dear chap, is that!

(GILBERT exits. CARTE looks at SULLIVAN, who shrugs.)

CARTE. Sometimes, he has the disposition of an untipped waiter. Thank God I don't have to spend that much time with him.

SULLIVAN. Can you appreciate what I go through?

CARTE. It's a cross we have to bear.

SULLIVAN. I wouldn't have it any other way. Every other collaborator I ever worked with was pleasant and friendly. They were also boring and totally without talent. It's a small price to pay.

(Go to black. Stage revolves. Music 6B: Partial Overture from "Pirates of Penzance" is heard. Lights up to reveal... Int. 5th Avenue Theatre—New York City—Dec. 31, 1879—afternoon. Set of The Pirates of Penzance. *A rocky seashore on the coast of Cornwall. In the distance is a calm sea on which a schooner lies at anchor. All actors onstage in rehearsal clothes move into position. The only way we might discern they are pirates is by the bandanas, swords, etc. As this sequence unfolds, actors will don more clothes [brought on by male and female TAILORS] until they are fully costumed at the conclusion. CARTE and GILBERT enter. GILBERT blows his whistle.)*

GILBERT *(to cast).* We've no time for a complete dress rehearsal, nor do we have all of the costumes. *(To the frantic TAILORS.)* I trust they will be in place for our eight o'clock curtain?

MALE TAILOR *(Brooklyn accent).* Oh yeah, Mr. Gilbert. It's just that the fabric wasn't ready, and the buttons are the wrong size and...

GILBERT *(cuts him off)*. Spare me! There are not enough crutches in this world for all the lame excuses! Just get it done. *(To cast.)* Mr. Sullivan, as you can see, is conspicuous by his absence. The result of having left half the music in England. He is, at this very moment, feverishly combing his memory and rewriting the arrangements and should arrive presently. *(Looks over cast.)* Blanche?

(A very attractive young woman presents herself. This is BLANCHE ROOSEVELT. And she should be played by the actress who plays MRS. GILBERT. The reason will be obvious soon enough.)

BLANCHE. Yes, Mr. Gilbert?

(GILBERT puts his arm around her waist, takes her aside. He is quite charming with her and the attraction is evident.)

GILBERT *(softly)*. Blanche, dear, you're doing a splendid job in the role and I expect you'll walk off with the lioness' share of the notices. Just remember to be deadly serious, won't you?

BLANCHE. Yes, Mr. Gilbert.

GILBERT. Not to worry if you don't see me this evening in the audience. First nights are too much agony and apprehension for my delicate psyche. After the show, however, perhaps you and I could have a bit of dinner and champagne in my suite and ... discuss your interpretation.

BLANCHE. Yes, Mr. Gilbert.

GILBERT. Good. I *like* a woman who expresses herself freely. *(Pats her on the behind and she returns to the cast upstage.)*

(CARTE approaches GILBERT, speaks quietly.)

CARTE. She's the mistress of Guy De Maupessant and *he* has the temperament of a cobra.

GILBERT. Yes, but *he* is in Paris and *we* are in New York and I doubt if his fangs are that long.

CARTE. It's a dangerous policy, William.

GILBERT *(sighs)*. I can't resist it from time to time. She reminds me of Kitten, whom I married when she was only seventeen. I've always been fatally attracted to women who look like my wife.

CARTE. Wouldn't it be easier to give all your affection to Mrs. Gilbert and leave the rest of womankind alone?

GILBERT. Ah ... well, yes. But you're talking *logic*. My problem is that I am one of those unfortunate men who believe that there is nothing above and beyond the call ... of beauty. *(Blows whistle.)* Enter the Pirate King! All others offstage!

(MUSIC 7: "I AM A PIRATE KING")

PIRATE KING (BARRINGTON).

OH, BETTER FAR TO LIVE AND DIE,
UNDER THE BRAVE BLACK FLAG I FLY,
THAN PLAY A SANCTIMONIOUS PART,
WITH A PIRATE HEAD AND A PIRATE HEART,
AWAY TO THE CHEATING WORLD GO YOU,
WHERE PIRATES ALL ARE WELL-TO-DO,
BUT I'LL BE TRUE TO THE SONG I SING,
AND LIVE AND DIE A PIRATE KING!
FOR I AM A PIRATE KING!

CHORUS.

YOU ARE!
HURRAH FOR OUR PIRATE KING!

PIRATE KING.

AND IT IS, IT IS A GLORIOUS THING
TO BE A PIRATE KING!

CHORUS.

IT IS!
HURRAH! HURRAH FOR OUR PIRATE KING!
HURRAH FOR THE PIRATE KING!

PIRATE KING.

WHEN I SALLY FORTH TO SEEK MY PREY,
I HELP MYSELF IN A ROYAL WAY,
I SINK A FEW MORE SHIPS, IT'S TRUE,
THAN A WELL-BRED MONARCH OUGHT TO DO.
BUT MANY A KING ON A FIRST-CLASS THRONE,
IF HE WANTS TO CALL HIS CROWN HIS OWN,
MUST MANAGE SOMEHOW TO GET THROUGH,
MORE DIRTY WORK THAN E'ER I DO!
FOR I AM A PIRATE KING...

CHORUS.

YOU ARE!
HURRAH FOR OUR PIRATE KING!

PIRATE KING.

AND IT IS, IT IS A GLORIOUS THING
TO BE A PIRATE KING!

CHORUS.

IT IS!

HURRAH FOR OUR PIRATE KING!
HURRAH FOR OUR PIRATE KING!

(Song ends. GILBERT enters.)

GILBERT. Very good, but be careful on the "brave, black flag I fly." I know it's difficult to sing those words but *I* like them so the problem is now *yours. (Shouts offstage.)* Mabel and sisters in place, please.

(PIRATES move off to one side to keep being fitted by TAILORS. MABEL [BLANCHE] and her SISTERS enter.)

GILBERT. Kindly begin at the recitative, Blanche. We'll do two choruses, the aria and finish with a restatement of the first five lines. I would have liked to have written more lyrics but I frankly couldn't think of anything further to say, so you'll just have to sing the same words and make them *sound* differently. If that makes no sense to you at all, don't question it. Just *do it!*

(MUSIC 8: "POOR WANDERING ONE")

MABEL.
POOR WANDERING ONE,
THOUGH THOU HAST SURELY STRAYED,
TAKE HEART OF GRACE,
THY STEPS RETRACE,
POOR WANDERING ONE...
POOR WANDERING ONE,
IF SUCH POOR LOVE AS MINE,
CAN HELP THEE FIND,

TRUE PEACE OF MIND,
WHY, TAKE IT, IT IS THINE.

SISTERS.

TAKE HEART, NO DANGERS LOW'RS
TAKE ANY HEART BUT OURS.

MABEL.

TAKE HEART, FAIR DAYS WILL SHINE,
TAKE ANY HEART, TAKE MINE.

SISTERS.

TAKE HEART, NO DANGERS LOW'RS
TAKE ANY HEART BUT OURS.

MABEL.

TAKE HEART, FAIR DAYS WILL SHINE,
TAKE ANY HEART, TAKE MINE.

(Wordless aria.)

POOR WANDERING ONE,
THOUGH THOU HAST SURELY STRAYED,
TAKE HEART OF GRACE,
THY STEPS RETRACE,
POOR WANDERING ONE.

(Wordless aria. SISTERS counterpoint.)

POOR WANDERING ONE
POOR WANDERING ONE
TAKE HEART, TAKE HEART

TAKE ANY HEART BUT OURS.
TAKE HEART, TAKE HEART

TAKE HEART, NO DANGER LOW'RS
TAKE ANY HEART BUT OURS.
TAKE HEART, TAKE HEART
TAKE ANY HEART BUT OURS.

(Song ends. GILBERT approaches BLANCHE, applauding loudly.)

GILBERT. Marvelous, absolutely splendid. Just a tiny bit *more* of *Carmen* and a little bit *less* of *The Barber of Seville* and we'll have it. *(He turns to see ...)*

(SULLIVAN enters, his arms laden with music paper. A few actors race to his side, to relieve him of the burden. SULLIVAN flops in a seat that is provided for him. GILBERT rushes to his side, concerned.)

GILBERT. You look unequivocally wretched, old fellow.

SULLIVAN. And I *feel* infinitely *worse* than I *look.* All that sea air did was give me a cold.

GILBERT. Can I get you something?

SULLIVAN. Three glorious months on the Riviera would be an excellent prescription. Can you arrange that?

GILBERT. 'Fraid not. Will you be able to conduct tonight?

SULLIVAN. Doubtful.

GILBERT. If you would but plan ahead instead of always having to rush your work at the conclusion, a great deal of the pressure might be off. Between dining with Dickens and comparing notes with Rossini, you hardly have a moment for...

SULLIVAN. I already have a mother who tells me that!

GILBERT. Well! If you want to take an attitude like...

SULLIVAN *(cuts him off)*. What time is it in England?

GILBERT *(looks at pocket watch)*. Four twenty in the afternoon.

SULLIVAN. Then the performance is on at Paignton.

GILBERT. Yes, and we can only hope it goes better than the anarchy we are about to present here tonight. *(Beat.)* Look, all I request is that you pay the same attention to the music as I do to the book and lyrics. I am always on time and you leave everything to the last minute. People have taken to calling you "The Late Arthur Sullivan."

SULLIVAN. In my condition, they're not far from wrong. I am not an organ grinder who turns a handle and disgorges music of any mood to order. Now, kindly leave me be! You have the melodies, the actors are waiting and the time is ticking.

GILBERT. Quite right. *(Shouts.)* George Grossmith!

(GROSSMITH enters, wearing a red military costume and a pith helmet [oversize] that almost covers his face. Must be comical entrance.)

GILBERT. George...what is that...*thing* on your head?

GROSSMITH. A pith helmet, sir.

GILBERT *(beat)*. Good taste prevents me from making any comment! Kindly remove that and commence your solo. *(Mutters to himself.)* Pith indeed. Looks more like... shhhh, quiet, everyone. *(Aloud.)* Begin, George!

(GILBERT steps to R at SULLIVAN's side [who remains seated] and they watch.)

(MUSIC 9: "I AM THE VERY MODEL")

MAJOR-GENERAL.

I AM THE VERY MODEL OF A MODERN MAJOR-GENERAL,
I'VE INFORMATION VEGETABLE, ANIMAL AND MINERAL,
I KNOW THE KINGS OF ENGLAND,
AND I QUOTE THE FIGHTS HISTORICAL,
FROM MARATHON TO WATERLOO,
IN ORDER CATEGORICAL.
I'M VERY WELL ACQUAINTED, TOO,
WITH MATTERS MATHEMATICAL.
I UNDERSTAND EQUATIONS,
BOTH THE SIMPLE AND QUADRATICAL,
ABOUT BINOMIAL THEOREM,
I'M TEEMING WITH A LOT O' NEWS,

Hmm ... a lot o' news, a lot o' news ... hmmm, difficult. Aha! I have it!

WITH MANY CHEERFUL FACTS ABOUT
THE SQUARE OF THE HYPOTENUSE!

CHORUS.

WITH MANY CHEERFUL FACTS
ABOUT THE SQUARE OF THE HYPOTNUSE!
WITH MANY CHEERFUL FACTS
ABOUT THE SQUARE OF THE HYPOTENUSE!
WITH MANY CHEERFUL FACTS
ABOUT THE SQUARE OF THE HYPOTENUSE...
HY-POT-E-POT-E-NUSE

MAJOR-GENERAL.

I'M VERY GOOD AT INTEGRAL AND DIFFERENTIAL CALCULUS
I KNOW THE SCIENTIFIC NAMES
OF BEINGS ANIMALCULOUS.
IN SHORT, IN MATTERS VEGETABLE, ANIMAL AND MINERAL,
I AM THE VERY MODEL OF A MODERN MAJOR-GENERAL!

CHORUS.

IN SHORT, IN MATTERS VEGETABLE, ANIMAL AND MINERAL,
HE IS THE VERY MODEL OF A MODERN MAJOR-GENERAL!

MAJOR-GENERAL.

I KNOW OUR MYTHIC HISTORY,
KING ARTHUR'S AND SIR CARADOC'S,
I ANSWER HARD ACROSTICS,
I'VE A PRETTY TASTE FOR PARADOX,
I QUOTE, IN ELEGIACS,
ALL THE CRIMES OF HELIOGABALUS,
IN CONICS, I CAN FLOOR
PECULIARITIES PARABOLOUS.
I CAN TELL UNDOUBTED RAPHAELS
FROM GERALD DOWS AND ZOFFANIES.
I KNOW THE CROAKING CHORUS
FROM THE "FROGS" OF ARISTOPHANES.
THEN I CAN HUM A FUGUE
OF WHICH I'VE HEARD THE MUSIC'S DIN AFORE

Ohhhh, dinafore, dinafore, that's almost impossible but ... yes! The answer is ...

AND WHISTLE ALL THE AIRS
FROM THAT INFERNAL NONSENSE PINAFORE!

CHORUS.

AND WHISTLE ALL THE AIRS
FROM THAT INFERNAL NONSENSE PINAFORE!
AND WHISTLE ALL THE AIRS
FROM THAT INFERNAL NONSENSE PINAFORE!
AND WHISTLE ALL THE AIRS
FROM THAT INFERNAL NONSENSE PINAPINAFORE!

MAJOR-GENERAL.

THEN I CAN WRITE A WASHING BILL
IN BABYLONIC CUNEIFORM.
AND TELL YOU EVERY DETAIL
OF CARACTACUS'S UNIFORM.
IN SHORT, IN MATTERS VEGETABLE, ANIMAL AND MINERAL,
I AM THE VERY MODEL OF A MODERN MAJOR-GENERAL!

CHORUS.

IN SHORT, IN MATTERS VEGETABLE, ANIMAL AND MINERAL
HE IS THE VERY MODEL OF A MODERN MAJOR-GENERAL.

MAJOR-GENERAL.

IN FACT, WHEN I KNOW WHAT IS MEANT
BY "MAMELON" AND "RAVELIN"
WHEN I CAN TELL, AT SIGHT,
A MAUSER RIFLE FROM JAVELIN,
WHEN SUCH AFFAIRS AS SORTIES
AND SURPRISES I'M MORE WARY AT,

AND WHEN I KNOW PRECISELY
WHAT IS MEANT BY "COMMISSARIAT"
WHEN I HAVE LEARNED WHAT PROGRESS
HAS BEEN MADE IN MODERN GUNNERY,
WHEN I KNOW MORE OF TACTICS
THAN A NOVICE IN A NUNNERY,
IN SHORT, WHEN I'VE A SMATTERING
OF ELEMENTAL STRATEGY...

Ohhh, now I've done it! What a predicament!
No rhyme at all. Strategy ... latigee,
catagee ... Aha! Simplicity itself.

YOU'LL SAY A BETTER MAJOR-GENERAL
HAS NEVER "SAT A GEE"!

CHORUS.

YOU'LL SAY A BETTER MAJOR-GENERAL
HAS NEVER "SAT A GEE"
YOU'LL SAY A BETTER MAJOR-GENERAL
HAS NEVER "SAT A GEE"
YOU'LL SAY A BETTER MAJOR-GENERAL
HAS NEVER SAT A "SAT A GEE"

MAJOR-GENERAL.

FOR MY MILITARY KNOWLEDGE
THOUGH I'M PLUCKY AND ADVENTURY,
HAS ONLY BEEN BROUGHT DOWN
FROM THE BEGINNING OF THE CENTURY.
BUT STILL IN MATTERS VEGETABLE, ANIMAL AND MINERAL
I AM THE VERY MODEL OF A MODERN MAJOR-GENERAL

CHORUS.

BUT STILL IN MATTERS VEGETABLE, ANIMAL AND MINERAL
HE IS THE VERY MODEL OF A MODERN MAJOR-GENERAL!

(Song ends. GROSSMITH is totally out of breath. GILBERT moves to center stage. GROSSMITH walks UR. [just this side of exhaustion].)

GILBERT. Policemen onstage for the medley. *(Blows whistle.)*

(SULLIVAN gets out of his seat, approaches GILBERT.)

SULLIVAN. Do you mind if I ask you something?

GILBERT. Ask away.

SULLIVAN. Kindly explain what "sat a gee" means? It has bothered me ever since I first read the lyric and, frankly, I was too embarrassed to ask.

GILBERT. A "gee," as you well know, is another word for a horse. Therefore, it means sitting upon a horse. Simple, what?

SULLIVAN. No!

GILBERT. No?

SULLIVAN. So much of that song appears to be rhymes for rhyme's sake and I admit I was dazzled by your cleverness but "sat a gee" seems far too obscure for any English audience, much less an American one. Can you somehow ... alter "sat a gee"?

GILBERT *(seething)*. My dear Sullivan, with the greatest respect, I have *never* suggested *you* might use an E-Flat instead of an E! So don't tell *me* when to use a Gee!

SULLIVAN *(startled)*. Well, it's too fast. The audience will never be able to appreciate my music.

GILBERT *(with measured tones)*. In the beginning, while *you* were out gambling in France or dining in St. Petersburg with the Czar, or shooting grouse with the Duke of Edinburgh and his wife Louise ... in the beginning, there was the word, *my* word. I don't think it's fast enough! *(Shouts.)* George!

(A weary GROSSMITH staggers forward.)

GROSSMITH. Sir?

GILBERT. Take it again from "In fact when I know what is meant" and do it double quick.

GROSSMITH. But—

GILBERT. Or perhaps you would prefer the ribbon counter at Woolworth's?

(MUSIC 10: REPRISE "I AM THE VERY MODEL")

MAJOR-GENERAL *(twice as fast)*.

IN FACT, WHEN I KNOW WHAT IS MEANT
BY "MAMELON" AND "RAVELIN"
WHEN I CAN TELL, AT SIGHT,
A MAUSER RIFLE FROM A JAVELIN,
WHEN SUCH AFFAIRS AS SORTIES
AND SURPRISES I'M MORE WARY AT
AND WHEN I KNOW PRECISELY
WHAT IS MEANT BY "COMMISARIAT"
WHEN I HAVE LEARNED WHAT PROGRESS
HAS BEEN MADE IN MODERN GUNNERY,
WHEN I KNOW MORE OF TACTICS
THAN A NOVICE IN A NUNNERY

IN SHORT, WHEN I'VE A SMATTERING
OF ELEMENTAL STRATEGY
YOU'LL SAY A BETTER MAJOR-GENERAL HAS NEVER
"SAT A GEE"!
FOR MY MILITARY KNOWLEDGE,
THOUGH I'M PLUCKY AND ADVENTURY
HAS ONLY BEEN BROUGHT DOWN
FROM THE BEGINNING OF THE CENTURY,
BUT STILL IN MATTERS VEGETABLE, ANIMAL, AND MINERAL
I AM THE VERY MODEL OF A MODERN MAJOR-GENERAL.

(GROSSMITH finishes, falls straight back in a faint and is caught by the other actors. GILBERT walks to him, stands over the unconscious man, smiles.)

GILBERT. Scintillating! *(To another actor.)* Drag him off, give him some brandy and bring on the police!

(GROSSMITH is seated DR and handed a brandy flask. Enter POLICE, marching in single file. They form in line, face the audience, led by large SERGEANT. MABEL waits nearby.)

(MUSIC 11: "WHEN THE FOEMAN BARES HIS STEEL")

SERGEANT *(POLICEMEN sing "Tarantara").*
WHEN THE FOEMAN BARES HIS STEEL,

CHORUS.
TARANTARA, TARANTARA!

SERGEANT.

WE UNCOMFORTABLE FEEL,

CHORUS.

TARANTARA!

SERGEANT.

AND WE FIND THE WISEST THING,

CHORUS.

TARANTARA, TARANTARA!

SERGEANT.

IS TO SLAP OUR CHESTS AND SING,

ALL.

TARANTARA!

SERGEANT.

FOR WHEN THREATENED BY EMEUTES,

CHORUS.

TARANTARA, TARANTARA!

SERGEANT.

AND YOUR HEART IS IN YOUR BOOTS,

CHORUS.

TARANTARA!

SERGEANT.

THERE IS NOTHING BRINGS IT 'ROUND,
LIKE THE TRUMPET'S MARTIAL SOUND.

ALL.

TARANTARA *(Sixteen times.)*

MABEL & WOMEN.

GO, YE HEROES, GO TO GLORY,
THOUGH YOU DIE IN COMBAT GORY,
YE SHALL LIVE IN SONG AND STORY.
GO TO IMMORTALITY!
GO TO DEATH, AND GO TO SLAUGHTER,
DIE, AND EVERY CORNISH DAUGHTER
WITH HER TEARS YOUR GRAVE SHALL WATER.
GO, YE HEROES, GO AND DIE!
GO, YE HEROES, GO AND DIE!
GO, YE HEROES, GO AND DIE!

SERGEANT *(POLICE sing "Tarantara")*.

THOUGH TO US, IT'S EVIDENT
TARANTARA, TARANTARA!
THESE ATTRACTIONS ARE WELL MEANT,
TARANTARA!
SUCH EXPRESSIONS DON'T APPEAR,
TARANTARA, TARANTARA!
CALCULATED MEN TO CHEER,
TARANTARA!
WHO ARE GOING TO MEET THEIR FATE,
IN A HIGHLY NERVOUS STATE,
TARANTARA, TARANTARA, TARANTARA!
STILL TO US IT'S EVIDENT,
THESE ATTENTIONS ARE WELL-MEANT,
TARANTARA, TARANTARA, TARANTARA!

EDITH *(a SISTER)*.

GO AND DO YOUR BEST ENDEAVOUR,
AND, BEFORE ALL LINKS WE SEVER,

WE WILL SAY FAREWELL FOREVER,
GO TO GLORY AND THE GRAVE
GO TO GLORY AND THE GRAVE

CHORUS *(female).*
FOR YOUR FOES ARE FIERCE AND RUTHLESS,
FALSE, UNMERCIFUL, AND COUTHLESS
YOUNG AND TENDER, OLD AND TOOTHLESS,
ALL IN VAIN THEIR MERCY CRAVE

(GILBERT enters, clapping his hands to stop the song.)

GILBERT. Good, good, we don't have enough time to finish so I pray you will all remember what you must do. Mainly, never forget that grimaces are derogatory to the comic actor's art. There must be no exaggeration in costume, makeup or demeanor. Got that? *(To SULLIVAN.)* Well, what'd you think?

SULLIVAN. Too many words.

GILBERT. Odd, I was of the opinion there was too much music. *(To cast.)* Make a note in your scripts. The line "false, unmerciful and couthless" should be changed to "false, unmerciful and truthless." I thought I could get an extra bit of fun in there but it goes by too quickly, and no one will appreciate it. Women, take a few minutes off to adjust your unmentionables. Police, go directly to the song which will make you all famous. And if you haven't guessed which song that is, you're in the wrong profession.

(MUSIC 12: "A POLICEMAN'S LOT")

SERGEANT.

WHEN A FELON'S NOT ENGAGED IN HIS EMPLOYMENT,

POLICE.

HIS EMPLOYMENT!

SERGEANT.

OR MATURING HIS FELONIOUS LITTLE PLANS.

POLICE.

LITTLE PLANS!

SERGEANT.

HIS CAPACITY FOR INNOCENT ENJOYMENT,

POLICE.

'CENT ENJOYMENT!

SERGEANT.

IS JUST AS GREAT AS ANY HONEST MAN'S!

POLICE.

HONEST MAN'S!

SERGEANT.

OUR FEELINGS WE WITH DIFFICULTY SMOTHER,

POLICE.

'CULTY SMOTHER!

SERGEANT.

WHEN CONSTABULARY DUTY'S TO BE DONE.

POLICE.

TO BE DONE!

SERGEANT.

AH, TAKE ONE CONSIDERATION WITH ANOTHER,

POLICE.

WITH ANOTHER!

SERGEANT.

A POLICEMAN'S LOT IS NOT A HAPPY ONE.

POLICE *(plus SERGEANT)*.

WHEN CONSTABULARY DUTY'S TO BE DONE,
TO BE DONE,
A POLICEMAN'S LOT IS NOT A HAPPY ONE,
HAPPY ONE!

SERGEANT.

WHEN THE ENTERPRISING BURGLAR'S NOT A-BURGLING,

POLICE.

NOT A-BURGLING!

SERGEANT.

WHEN THE CUT-THROAT ISN'T OCCUPIED IN CRIME,

POLICE.
'PIED IN CRIME!

SERGEANT.
HE LOVES TO HEAR THE LITTLE BROOK A-GURGLING,

POLICE.
BROOK A-GURGLING!

SERGEANT.
AND LISTEN TO THE MERRY VILLAGE CHIME.

POLICE.
VILLAGE CHIME!

SERGEANT.
WHEN THE COSTER'S FINISHED JUMPING ON HIS MOTHER,

POLICE.
ON HIS MOTHER

SERGEANT.
HE LOVES TO LIE A-BASKING IN THE SUN

POLICE.
IN THE SUN!

SERGEANT.
AH, TAKE ONE CONSIDERATION WITH ANOTHER,

POLICE.
WITH ANOTHER!

SERGEANT.
A POLICEMAN'S LOT IS NOT AN 'APPY ONE!

SERGEANT & POLICE.
A POLICEMAN'S LOT IS NOT AN 'APPY ONE
'APPY ONE.

(Song ends. CARTE enters.)

CARTE. I've been quietly watching from the rear of the theatre.

GILBERT *(snappish)*. Kindly keep your comments to yourself.

CARTE. It looks wonderful.

GILBERT *(melts)*. Tell me more.

CARTE. I haven't a word of criticism.

SULLIVAN. Good. Most criticism consists in finding hidden meaning in a play that the authors never knew was there. May I leave now?

GILBERT. Yes, by all means, my dear fellow. Go back to the hotel, have a nap, have some champagne. As usual, I won't be here until after the performance.

CARTE. New York isn't London, William. I wouldn't advise you to walk the streets here.

GILBERT. Bosh. The only persons I have to fear are Broadway producers who might whack me over the head and try to torture me into giving them the libretto and the score.

CARTE. Nevertheless, caution should be exercised.

GILBERT. Double bosh. I'll merely tell them to buy a ticket, like everyone else. *(Walks to SULLIVAN, shakes his hand.)* Feel better, old man. I know you'll be well enough to conduct tonight. Break a baton!

(SULLIVAN smiles wanly, exits.)

GILBERT *(to cast)*. The last four pages, nonstop, and if anyone makes a mistake, don't think I didn't see it because I did.

(The actors, now all dressed in costume, begin moving to their places. CARTE and GILBERT come downstage, speak privately.)

GILBERT. What happens if we fail? What then?

CARTE. Do you really have any doubts about this?

GILBERT. Sullivan and I like to toss barbs at the critics but the truth is it's *they* who tell us if what *we* did is good. We're too close, the three of us to know.

CARTE. Do you like it?

GILBERT. Yes.

CARTE. Then it's good. You're Gilbert and Sullivan. If the unnamed *they* knew how to write and compose what you do, *they'd* be Gilbert and Sullivan.

GILBERT *(shakes his hand)*. I wish I had your confidence.

CARTE. Before we met, I had a string of failed plays I'd written ... I wish I had your talent.

(MABEL [BLANCHE] steps forward.)

BLANCHE. Ready, Mr. Gilbert.

GILBERT *(to the cast).* From the pirates' entrance. *(To BLANCHE.)* I've taken the liberty of ordering four ounces of caviar in my suite after the show. That's at least a year's work for a sturgeon. I hope you *like* caviar.

BLANCHE *(beat).* Uhmm... I'd prefer fish and chips.

GILBERT. Then *that's* what you shall have! Now! Back into line and let's make this rousing. And *you* may call me... Winkie.

(GENERAL's DAUGHTERS enter, dressed in white peignoirs, carry candles. Pirates kneel. POLICE stand over them triumphantly. POLICE, holding PIRATES by their collars, take out handkerchiefs, weep.)

(MUSIC 13: (FINALE} "TAKE HEART")

MAJOR-GENERAL.

AWAY WITH THEM, AND PLACE THEM AT THE BAR!

(RUTH enters.)

RUTH.

ONE MOMENT! LET ME TELL YOU WHO THEY ARE!
THEY ARE NO MEMBERS OF THE COMMON THRONG,
THEY ARE ALL NOBLEMEN WHO HAVE GONE WRONG

CHORUS OF GIRLS.

THEY ARE ALL NOBLEMEN WHO HAVE GONE WRONG

MAJOR-GENERAL.

NO ENGLISHMAN, UNMOVED, THAT STATEMENT HEARS.
BECAUSE, WITH ALL OUR FAULTS,
WE LOVE OUR HOUSE OF PEERS!
I PRAY YOU, PARDON ME, EX-PIRATE KING,
PEERS WILL BE PEERS AND YOUTH WILL HAVE ITS FLING.
RESUME YOUR RANKS AND LEGISLATIVE DUTIES,
AND TAKE MY DAUGHTERS, ALL OF WHOM ARE BEAUTIES!

MABEL.

POOR WONDERING ONES,
THOUGH YE HAVE SURELY STRAYED
TAKE HEART OF GRACE,
YOUR STEPS RETRACE,
POOR WONDERING ONES...
POOR WANDERING ONES,
IF SUCH POOR LOVE AS OURS,
CAN HELP YOU FIND
TRUE PEACE OF MIND,
WHY TAKE IT, IT IS YOURS!

(Simultaneously with others).

AH, AH, AH, AH, AH, AH, AH, AH, AH, FAIR DAYS WILL SHINE
TAKE HEART,
TAKE MINE!
TAKE HEART,
TAKE MINE!
HEART, FAIR DAYS WILL SHINE, TAKE HEART,
FAIR DAYS WILL SHINE,
TAKE HEART,
TAKE HEART, TAKE OURS!

MEN/WOMEN	CHORUS
POOR WAND'RING ONE!	**POOR WAND'RING ONE!**
POOR WAND'RING ONE!	**POOR WAND'RING ONE!**
FAIR DAYS WILL SHINE;	

MEN/WOMEN/CHORUS.

TAKE HEART, TAKE HEART,
TAKE ANY HEART, TAKE OURS!
TAKE HEART,
TAKE OURS!
TAKE TAKE HEART,

ALL TOGETHER.

TAKE HEART, TAKE OURS!

CURTAIN – INTERVAL

(Barring any union interference, it would be pleasant if we were able to use the following songs from Patience, *This would be for two reasons: to delight the audience that remains in their seats, and to indicate the passage of time for those Savoyards who knew that* Patience *was the show between* Pirates *and* Iolanthe. *These should be pre-recorded or just done by alternate pianist so orchestra can take a break.)*

1. "I Cannot Tell What This Love May Be"– Patience Chorus.
2. "If You Want a Receipt"– Colonel, Dragoons.
3. "Silvered is the Raven Hair"– Patience, Bunthorne.
4. "It's Clear That Medieval Art"– Duke, Colonel, Bunthorne.
5. "When I Go Out of the Door"– Bunthorne, Grosvenor.
6. "Finale"—Ensemble.

END OF ACT ONE

ACT TWO

AT RISE: *Int. Backstage—Savoy Theatre—December 28, 1881—afternoon. The cast of* Patience *is onstage. The COLONEL and the CHORUS OF DRAGOONS. GILBERT and SULLIVAN watch from the wings.*

(MUSIC 14: "WHEN I FIRST PUT THIS UNIFORM ON")

COLONEL.

WHEN I FIRST PUT THIS UNIFORM ON
I SAID, AS I LOOKED IN THE GLASS
"IT'S ONE IN A MILLION
THAT ANY CIVILIAN
MY FIGURE AND FORM WILL SURPASS
GOLD LACE HAS A CHARM FOR THE FAIR
AND I'VE PLENTY OF THAT, AND TO SPARE
WHILE A LOVER'S PROFESSIONS,
WHEN UTTERED IN HESSIANS,
ARE ELOQUENT EVERYWHERE"
A FACT THAT I COUNTED UPON
WHEN I FIRST PUT THIS UNIFORM ON

DRAGOONS.

BY A SIMPLE COINCIDENCE, FEW
COULD EVER BE COUNTED UPON

THE SAME THING OCCURRED TO ME,
WHEN I FIRST PUT THIS UNIFORM ON

COLONEL.

I SAID, WHEN I FIRST PUT IT ON
"IT IS PLAIN TO THE VERIEST DUNCE
THAT EVERY BEAUTY
WILL FEEL IT HER DUTY
TO YIELD TO ITS GLAMOUR AT ONCE
THEY WILL SEE THAT I'M FREELY
GOLD-LACED
IN A UNIFORM HANDSOME AND CHASTE"
BUT THE PERIPATETICS
OF LONG-HAIRED AESTHETICS
ARE VERY MUCH MORE TO THEIR TASTE
WHICH I NEVER COUNTED UPON
WHEN I FIRST PUT THIS UNIFORM ON

DRAGOONS.

BY A SIMPLE COINCIDENCE, FEW
COULD EVER BE RECKONED UPON
I DIDN'T ANTICIPATE THAT
WHEN I FIRST PUT THIS UNIFORM ON

(Song ends. GILBERT and SULLIVAN step on stage.)

GILBERT. That was fantastically ... adequate. We've lots to do.

(D'OYLY CARTE enters.)

CARTE. In a moment, William. There's something I must clear up immediately.

GILBERT. As you wish, Carte. You have ninety seconds.

CARTE *(to the cast)*. Tonight marks the first performance of *Patience* here at the Savoy under electric lights. It is also what we pray will be the first of many thousands of performances of my partners' works. Everyone who matters will be here, including the Prince of Wales.

(Cast murmurs at the thought.)

CARTE. I know some of you have expressed trepidation over the new system. May I assure you that there is absolutely no danger to life or limb with this revolutionary process.

(Actor raises hand.)

CARTE. Yes, Albert?

ALBERT. A friend of mine told me about a friend of *his* who heard that somebody was electrocuted by one of those things.

CARTE. Silly rumors, thrice removed. Let me prove a point. *(Offstage shout.)* Mr. Turer!

(Stagehand enters carrying a light bulb attached to a long cord. It is lit. He hands it to CARTE who wraps it in his silk handkerchief. The stagehand offers CARTE a small hammer.)

CARTE *(covering the action)*. Mr. Thomas Edison of the United States has harnessed this remarkable energy source and I predict it will eventually replace the old-fashioned and somewhat odorous gas lighting we've had to use until now. *(He holds the hammer over the bulb, the actors shrink back.)* You can move in.

(They inch in. CARTE smashes the bulb, the actors oooooh and ahhhh. CARTE pulls the handkerchief off the bulb.)

CARTE. As you can see, not a singe. We may experience a popped bulb during the performance but there is nothing to fear.

GILBERT. Except for getting their lines right due to the new surroundings. How much time have we?

SULLIVAN. Twelve minutes before their dinner break.

GILBERT. I'll never understand how performers can eat before a show. No great singing was ever done on a full stomach.

SULLIVAN. They have a union now.

GILBERT. Yes, which means they do *less*, have *more* time to do it in and want to get more pay for *not* doing it!

(MRS. RONALDS and MRS. GILBERT enter.)

SULLIVAN. We'll be with you, presently, ladies.

(Cast is annoyed, shows it by moving very slowly.)

GILBERT. Do I detect a bit of recalcitrance? Remember this, my adorable cast, one can never have too much real estate, too much honor or ...

CAST. Too much rehearsal.

(They continue moving into place. GILBERT, SULLIVAN, FANNY RONALDS and KITTEN GILBERT cross DR. CARTE follows.)

GILBERT *(sotto voce)*. I've never really liked this show. No one understands the aesthetic movement, not even the aesthetics themselves.

SULLIVAN. Well, I think it's the best music I've done to date but you *are* right. If we're to do any business in the United States at all, we'll have to come up with some huge idea to boost the box office.

KITTEN. I think it's delightful.

GILBERT. Yes, but you think *everything* I do is delightful so that hardly can be counted as an objective opinion.

FANNY. Perhaps that's why you've stayed married for so many years.

GILBERT *(squeezes his wife at waist)*. It's only one of many reasons. *(To SULLIVAN.)* This opera, more than any other, is a triumph of *your* music over *my* lyrics.

SULLIVAN. I assume that is a compliment?

GILBERT. Of course it is!

SULLIVAN. Then thank you. I took music theory in the same room where Bach wrote all of his works in Leipzig so you can imagine how the room was impregnated with fugue and counterpoint.

(GILBERT, KITTEN and CARTE look at one another for a long beat. They haven't a clue of what SULLIVAN is speaking about. Finally...)

CARTE. I have an idea.

(The foursome turn their heads, as one, to hear what CARTE has to say. Their expressions instantly indicate that they probably won't like his suggestion.)

CARTE. The aesthetic movement is, after all, about Whistler and Ruskin and Oscar Wilde and Rosetti and whatever it is they're prattling on about.

SULLIVAN. So?

CARTE. So I'm going to schedule a tour for one of them at the same time we open in New York. Sort of softening the American intellect in preparation for our show.

SULLIVAN. I should think the American intellect is soft enough already.

GILBERT. Impossible! They would *never* betray their principles for something as common as money.

(OSCAR WILDE enters, wears a velvet suit, carries a lily. He is effete, snippy and ... well, he is OSCAR WILDE.)

WILDE. What, never?

SULLIVAN. Well, *hardly* ever.

(SULLIVAN moves to WILDE. Shakes his hand heartily. GILBERT and CARTE follow. The WOMEN stay put. The cast, still upstage, will respond with laughter and even polite applause at the mots tossed back and forth by WILDE and GILBERT.)

SULLIVAN. Hello, Oscar. *(Indicates others.)* Mrs. Ronalds, Mrs. Gilbert, you know Carte and this is ...

WILDE. Don't bother, Arthur. I never remember anyone's name anymore. It's much easier to call men "sir" and women "madam." Except, of course, for madams. *Their* names I can *always* remember.

GILBERT *(miffed)*. I am William Gilbert.

WILDE. Of course you are. I am a great admirer of yours... perhaps not as great as *you* are, but you may count me among the thousands in second place for your affections.

CARTE. Oscar is going to do our lecture tour, aren't you, Oscar?

WILDE. If the money is sufficient, I will speak to Aborigines, Austrians, even Americans. And I shall be most sincere, even if they don't understand a word I say. For when it comes to sincerity, style is everything. *(Beat.)* Hmmm, I must use that sometime.

(CARTE and SULLIVAN enjoy the by-play between these two wordsmiths.)

GILBERT. Do you ever give your tongue a rest and listen? A good listener is not only a much sought after dinner guest—after a while, he *learns* something.

WILDE. Listening is an overrated attribute. Instead of listening to what *you* are saying, I find myself already listening to what *I* am about to say.

GILBERT. I wish I could speak the way you do, Mr. Wilde. Then I would keep my mouth shut and claim it as a virtue.

WILDE. Ah, but that would be selfish. I could, of course, deny *myself* the pleasure of talking but not to others the pleasure of hearing my words.

CARTE *(looks at watch)*. Four minutes until dinner.

WILDE *(to SULLIVAN)*. Does he announce *all* his meals that way?

GILBERT. Have you seen this show?

WILDE. I never go to the theatre. If it achieves bad notices, the show usually closes before I get there and if it merits good notices, the place is too crowded with shopkeepers and tourists.

GILBERT *(shouts)*. Bunthorne!

(BARRINGTON [as BUNTHORNE] steps forward. He wears a velvet suit exactly like WILDE's and also carries a lily.)

BUNTHORNE. Sir?

GILBERT. Sing the song we wrote about Mr. Wilde.

BUNTHORNE. You ... want me ... to sing the song in front of *him*?

WILDE. Go ahead, please. I won't bite you, young man, appetizing though it might be.

GILBERT *(to pit)*. Music!

(As BUNTHORNE gets into it, he becomes more confident, especially since nobody is enjoying it half as much as WILDE, who keeps time, smiles and, in general, is having marvelous fun.)

(MUSIC 15: "IF YOU'RE ANXIOUS")

BUNTHORNE.

AM I ALONE,
AND UNOBSERVED? I AM!

THEN LET ME OWN,
***I'M* AN AESTHETIC SHAM!**
THIS AIR SEVERE,
IS BUT A MERE VENEER!
THIS CYNIC *SMILE*
IS BUT A WILE OF GUILE!
THIS COSTUME CHASTE
IS BUT GOOD TASTE MISPLACED!
***LET* ME CONFESS!**
A LANGUID LOVE FOR LILIES DOES *NOT* BLIGHT ME,
LANK LIMBS AND HAGGARD CHEEKS DO *NOT* DELIGHT ME.
I DO *NOT* CARE FOR DIRTY GREENS BY ANY MEANS,
I DO *NOT* LONG FOR ALL ONE SEES THAT'S JAPANESE,
I AM *NOT* FOND OF UTTERING PLATITUDES,
IN STAINED-GLASS ATTITUDES.
IN SHORT, MY MEDIAEVALISM'S AFFECTATION,
BORN OF A MORBID LOVE OF ADMIRATION.
IF YOU'RE ANXIOUS FOR TO SHINE,
IN THE HIGH AESTHETIC LINE,
AS A MAN OF CULTURE RARE,
YOU MUST GET UP ALL THE GERMS,
OF THE TRANSCENDENTAL TERMS,
AND PLANT THEM EVERYWHERE!
YOU MUST LIE UPON THE DAISIES,
AND DISCOURSE IN NOVEL PHRASES,
OF YOUR COMPLICATED STATE OF MIND.
THE MEANING DOESN'T MATTER,
IF IT'S ONLY IDLE CHATTER,
OF A TRANSCENDENTAL KIND!
AND EVERYONE WILL SAY,

AS YOU WALK YOUR MYSTIC WAY...
"IF THIS YOUNG MAN EXPRESSES HIMSELF
IN TERMS TOO DEEP FOR ME,
WHY, WHAT A VERY SINGULARLY DEEP YOUNG MAN
THIS DEEP YOUNG MAN MUST BE!"
BE ELOQUENT IN PRAISE
OF THE VERY DULL OLD DAYS
WHICH HAVE LONG SINCE PASSED AWAY,
AND CONVINCED 'EM, IF YOU CAN,
THAT THE REIGN OF GOOD QUEEN ANNE
WAS CULTURE'S PALMIEST DAY.
OF COURSE, YOU WILL POOH-POOH
WHATEVER'S FRESH AND NEW,
AND DECLARE IT'S CRUDE AND MEAN,
FOR ART STOPPED SHORT
IN THE CULTIVATED COURT
OF THE EMPRESS JOSEPHINE.
AND EVERYONE WILL SAY,
AS YOU WALK YOUR MYSTIC WAY...
"IF THAT'S GOOD ENOUGH FOR HIM
WHICH IS GOOD ENOUGH FOR ME,
WHY WHAT A VERY CULTIVATED KIND OF YOUTH
THIS KIND OF YOUTH MUST BE."
WHEN A SENTIMENTAL PASSION
OF A VEGETABLE FASHION
MUST EXCITE YOUR LANGUID SPLEEN
AN ATTACHMENT, À LA PLATO
FOR A BASHFUL YOUNG POTATO
OR A NOT-TOO-FRENCH FRENCH BEAN
THOUGH THE PHILISTINES MAY JOSTLE
YOU WILL RANK AS AN APOSTLE
IN THE HIGH AESTHETIC BAND
IF YOU WALK DOWN PICCADILLY

WITH A POPPY OR A LILY
IN YOUR MEDIAEVAL HAND
AND EVERYONE WILL SAY
AS YOU WALK YOUR FLOW'RY WAY
"IF HE'S CONTENT WITH A VEGETABLE LOVE
WHICH WOULD CERTAINLY *NOT* SUIT ME
WHY WHAT A MOST PARTICULARLY PURE YOUNG MAN
THIS PURE YOUNG MAN MUST BE."

(Song ends. WILDE applauds loudest of all, plants a kiss on the singer's lips, stands back and bravos as stage revolves to: Int. Savoy Theatre, November 25, 1882—afternoon. The set of Iolanthe. *An Arcadian landscape. A faux river runs around the back of the stage. A rustic bridge crosses it. GILBERT and CARTE enter.)*

GILBERT. It's a magnificent idea, Carte, but I can't seem to convince Sullivan.

CARTE. Why bother even thinking about another show when we still haven't opened *Iolanthe*?

GILBERT. Because you, more than anyone, must realize that it takes a great many ticket sales to feed this grand white elephant you've built for us.

CARTE. White elephant indeed! It's a fantastic theatre with exceptional acoustics.

GILBERT. Yes, they *are* perfect. The actors onstage can hear every cough in the audience. But what if *Iolanthe* goes the way of our first show, *Thespis*?

CARTE. There's no comparison. That was underrehearsed, the singers had terrible voices, nobody knew anything about Greek gods ...

GILBERT. Even so, what if this play dies? Does the theatre sit empty or do we rent it out for a six-a-day vaudeville?

CARTE. Never! I always had a dream about English comic opera in a theatre devoted to that alone and I will not give up that dream. All right, all right. What's the idea?

GILBERT. I want to do a story about a magic lozenge that transforms people.

CARTE. Into what?

GILBERT. I haven't figured that out yet but I must get Sullivan to agree to the basic principle of the lozenge so I can begin to marshal my thoughts. Could you... *would* you talk to him about it?

CARTE. I'll see what I can do.

(SULLIVAN enters with MRS. RONALDS. His arms are filled with music.)

SULLIVAN. Good afternoon, gentlemen. Here are the final arrangements for the finale.

GILBERT *(looks at pocket watch)*. You're improving. We still have seven hours until we open for the critics.

SULLIVAN *(ignores that)*. I'm still not certain of the tempo you want on "When Britain ruled the waves." Can we discuss it for a moment?

GILBERT. Certainly.

(GILBERT and SULLIVAN move to UL, hold a conversation we cannot hear. MRS. RONALDS and CARTE cross DR. She looks over her shoulder at her beloved, talks softly to CARTE so SULLIVAN and GILBERT can't hear.)

FANNY. Arthur wants to quit.

CARTE *(thunderstruck)*. You can't be serious.

FANNY. He's tired and the pressure of having to do these shows and work with Gilbert is making him older by the minute.

CARTE. He needs a rest. We all do.

FANNY. It's more than that. His kidneys aren't functioning properly, he's finding it very difficult to deal with his mother's death and he does not enjoy writing this type of music.

CARTE. It has made him a rich man.

FANNY. We both know he's capable of better things. He wants to write operas, oratorios, music that will last. He's the first British composer who has been deemed worthy of following in Mendelssohn's footsteps but you'd never know it from plays like these.

CARTE. I've already said I'll build him an opera house as soon as the Savoy is paid for.

FANNY. He can't wait, Richard... he's only forty years old and he *looks* fifty and *feels* like seventy. This has to stop.

CARTE. Did *he* tell you to say this?

FANNY. No, but we've discussed it many times and...

(Her speech is interrupted by an argument that explodes between SULLIVAN and GILBERT.)

SULLIVAN. And *you* have made me feel like a rum-tiddy composer!

GILBERT. What on earth are you talking about?

SULLIVAN. Rum-tiddy, rum-tiddy melodies to serve your overwritten multiple rhymes. I'm sick of it!

GILBERT *(attempting to placate him).* My dear Sullivan, this is not grand opera, where the librettist must sacrifice himself on the altar of the composer.

SULLIVAN. And yet, *that's* what I've been doing for *you*! We're supposed to be a collaboration. That means Master and Master, not Master and servant.

GILBERT. These shows are not *mine*, with *your* music as an afterthought. We *are* a team. Before we began to work together, English comic opera had practically ceased to exist. We treated thoroughly farcical subjects in a thoroughly serious manner and gave it humor without heartlessness. *(Beat.)* Whatever you wish is yours.

SULLIVAN. All right... consult me before you draft the musical situations... ask my feelings about the staging... let me offer some comments about the singers' voices other than "um, very nice, indeed." I need to be part of it, right from the outset.

GILBERT. Done! Anything else?

SULLIVAN. The opportunity to write some beautiful ballads, some open-noted songs where I compose a proper melody and needn't perspire over each syllable.

GILBERT. And so you shall *have* that opportunity. The moment we begin our next show. *(Beat.)* The one about the magic lozenge.

SULLIVAN. Good lord, no!

GILBERT. But it's a capital idea. Perhaps my best yet.

SULLIVAN. It isn't an *idea*! It's a notion. And a terrible notion at that.

(The cast, in rehearsal clothes, enter. One of the women is the same actress who plays MRS. GILBERT and BLANCHE.)

GILBERT. We'll continue this discussion after awhile. *(To cast.)* Ladies and gentlemen. I am not pleased to say that things have been going far too well. It's axiomatic that good rehearsals usually mean a rotten performance. So I trust you will all do your best to catastrophise today's rehearsal, thus assuring me a good performance tonight, while I shall be walking the streets, in search of a heavenly answer as to why I ever left the law and got into this business in the first place.

(The cast, who listened apprehensively at first, are now laughing as they have caught onto GILBERT's kidding.)

GILBERT. In truth, these rehearsals, like almost all I have overseen, have been somewhere between a debacle and Armageddon. My collaborator was late with the music. The revised costumes are still being hemmed. The orchestra have no idea what the show is about and George Grossmith regards my book and lyrics as more of a blueprint than a building. George? Where are you?

(GROSSMITH, who was hiding in the rear, steps forward. He wears the outfit of a magistrate, replete with wig and robe.)

GROSSMITH. Yes, Mr. Gilbert?

GILBERT. Prepare yourself for your star turn. *(Moves to CARTE, indicates the actress who resembles KITTEN.)* That little one is a pip, isn't she?

CARTE. She's married.

GILBERT. So am I.

CARTE. To a difficult, jealous and sometimes violent mate.

GILBERT. So am I.

CARTE. You're not still at it, are you?

GILBERT. Unfortunately, no. My mind keeps making dates that my body can't keep. I'm starting to regret the sins I *didn't* commit. *(Looks at GROSSMITH.)* What are you waiting for, George?

SULLIVAN. He's waiting for *you.*

GILBERT. George, your diction gets better with each passing year.

GROSSMITH. And my voice?

SULLIVAN. It gets more ... interesting.

(MRS. RONALDS joins SULLIVAN, talks to GILBERT.)

FANNY. I'm always impressed with the way you research your work, William. Many of your lyrics could have been written by a barrister.

GILBERT. They were. I spent several dismal years attempting to make a living in court. I found the *study* of law to be exquisite, but the *practice* of it abominable.

FANNY. Do you agree with Shakespeare? First thing we do is kill the lawyers?

GILBERT. Not at all. Lawyers are a much-maligned group. Some of them will even tell the truth—but, of course, they'll do *anything* to win a case! *(To GROSSMITH.)* Are you rested, George? Is your mouth in fine fettle?

GROSSMITH. Never felt fettler.

GILBERT. This "Nightmare Song" is the single most difficult lyric *I've* ever written.

SULLIVAN. And the least melodious tune *I've* ever written.

GILBERT. Be that as it may, get on with it, George.

(NOTE: During the following, one of the stagehands will call SULLIVAN to the telephone at L. SULLIVAN will take the call, visibly pale, say something to MRS. RONALDS who will comfort him with her arms around his waist. This should be unobtrusive but noticeable. SULLIVAN will then exit. This will all occur during the song.)

(MUSIC 16: "THE NIGHTMARE SONG")

LORD CHANCELLOR.

WHEN YOU'RE LYING AWAKE
WITH A DISMAL HEADACHE
AND REPOSE IS TABOO'D BY ANXIETY,
I CONCEIVE YOU MAY USE
ANY LANGUAGE YOU CHOOSE
TO INDULGE IN, WITHOUT IMPROPRIETY.
FOR YOUR BRAIN IS ON FIRE,
THE BEDCLOTHES CONSPIRE
OF USUAL SLUMBER TO PLUNDER YOU;
FIRST YOUR COUNTERPANE GOES,
AND UNCOVERS YOUR TOES
***AND* YOUR SHEET SLIPS DEMURELY FROM UNDER YOU.**
THEN THE BLANKETING TICKLES
YOU FEEL LIKED MIXED PICKLES
SO TERRIBLY SHARP IS THE PRICKING,
AND YOU'RE HOT AND YOU'RE CROSS,
AND YOU TUMBLE AND TOSS,

TILL THERE'S NOTHING TWIXT YOU AND THE TICKING.
THEN THE BEDCLOTHES ALL CREEP
TO THE GROUND, IN A HEAP,
AND YOU PICK 'EM ALL UP IN A TANGLE,
NEXT YOUR PILLOW RESIGNS,
AND POLITELY DECLINES,
TO REMAIN AT ITS USUAL ANGLE.
WELL, YOU GET SOME REPOSE
IN THE FORM OF A DOZE,
WITH HOT EYE-BALLS AND HEAD EVER ACHING.
BUT YOUR SLUMBERING TEEMS
WITH SUCH HORRIBLE DREAMS,
THAT YOU'D VERY MUCH BETTER BE WAKING;
FOR YOU DREAM YOU ARE CROSSING
THE CHANNEL, AND TOSSING
ABOUT IN A STEAMER FROM HARWICH (HARRIDGE),
WHICH IS SOMETHING BETWEEN
A LARGE BATHING MACHINE
AND A VERY SMALL SECOND-CLASS CARRIAGE.
AND YOU'RE GIVING A TREAT
(PENNY ICE AND COLD MEAT)
TO A PARTY OF FRIENDS AND RELATIONS,
THEY'RE A RAVENOUS HORDE
AND THEY ALL CAME ON BOARD
AT SLOANE SQUARE AND SOUTH KENSINGTON STATIONS,
AND BOUND ON THAT JOURNEY
YOU FIND YOUR ATTORNEY
(WHO STARTED THAT MORNING FROM DEVON);
HE'S A BIT UNDERSIZED,

AND YOU DON'T FEEL SURPRISED
WHEN HE TELLS YOU HE'S ONLY ELEVEN.
WELL, YOU'RE DRIVING LIKE MAD
WITH THIS SINGULAR LAD
(BY THE WAY, THE SHIP'S NOW A
FOUR-WHEELER),
AND YOU'RE PLAYING ROUND GAMES
AND HE CALLS YOU BAD NAMES
WHEN YOU TELL HIM THAT "TIES PAY THE
DEALER"!
BUT THIS YOU CAN'T STAND,
SO YOU THROW UP YOUR HAND,
AND YOU FIND YOU'RE AS COLD AS AN ICICLE.
IN YOUR SHIRT AND YOUR SOCKS
(THE BLACK SILK WITH GOLD CLOCKS)
CROSSING SALISBURY PLAIN ON A BICYCLE:
AND HE AND THE CREW
ARE ON BICYCLES, TOO
WHICH THEY'VE SOMEHOW OR OTHER
INVESTED IN,
AND HE'S TELLING THE TARS
ALL THE PARTICULARS
OF A COMPANY HE'S INTERESTED IN
IT'S A SCHEME OF DEVICES,
TO GET AT LOW PRICES
ALL GOODS FROM COUGH MIXTURES TO
CABLES,
(WHICH TICKLED THE SAILORS)
BY TREATING RETAILERS
AS THOUGH THEY WERE ALL VEGETABLES.
YOU GET A GOOD SPADESMAN
TO PLANT A SMALL TRADESMAN,
(FIRST TAKE OFF HIS BOOTS WITH A
BOOT-TREE),
AND HIS LEGS WILL TAKE ROOT

AND HIS FINGERS WILL SHOOT,
AND THEY'LL BLOSSOM AND BUD LIKE A FRUIT-TREE.
FROM THE GREENGROCER TREE
YOU GET GRAPES AND GREEN PEA,
CAULIFLOWER, PINEAPPLE, AND CRANBERRIES,
WHILE THE PASTY COOK PLANT
CHERRY BRANDY WILL GRANT,
APPLE PUFFS, AND THREE CORNERS AND BANBURYS.
THE SHARES ARE A PENNY,
AND EVER SO MANY
ARE TAKEN BY ROTHSCHILD AND BARING,
AND JUST AS A FEW
ARE ALLOTTED TO YOU,
YOU AWAKE WITH A SHUDDER DESPAIRING...
YOU'RE A REGULAR WRECK WITH A CRICK IN YOUR NECK
AND NO WONDER YOU SNORE
FOR YOUR HEAD'S ON THE FLOOR,
AND YOU'VE NEEDLES AND PINS
FROM YOUR SOLES TO YOUR SHINS
AND YOUR FLESH IS A-CREEP,
FOR YOUR LEFT LEG'S ASLEEP,
AND YOU'VE CRAMP IN YOUR TOES,
AND A FLY ON YOUR NOSE,
AND SOME FLUFF IN YOUR LUNG,
AND A FEVERISH TONGUE,
AND A THIRST THAT'S INTENSE,
AND A GENERAL SENSE
THAT YOU HAVEN'T BEEN SLEEPING IN CLOVER.
BUT THE DARKNESS HAS PASSED,
AND IT'S DAYLIGHT AT LAST

AND THE NIGHT HAS BEEN LONG,
DITTO DITTO MY SONG
AND THANK GOODNESS,
THEY'RE BOTH OF THEM... OVER.

(Song ends. LORD CHANCELLOR [GROSSMITH] falls over in a faint. GILBERT approaches.)

GILBERT. The man is definitely out of condition.

GROSSMITH *(looks up, fear in his eyes).* Not faster? Please tell me, not faster...

GILBERT *(laughs).* No, George. No faster, I promise.

(He helps GROSSMITH to his feet and notices that SULLIVAN exits without saying another word. The actors in background move to different positions as GILBERT approaches MRS. RONALDS.)

GILBERT. There's something wrong. Don't deny it, Fanny. Sullivan always turns that peculiar shade of grey whenever there's a problem.

FANNY. I don't think he'd want me to tell you what it is.

GILBERT. Another death in the family?

FANNY. No, it's... it's...

GILBERT. Short of death, what other tragedy is there? *(No answer from FANNY.)* Fanny... we bicker, we battle, we demean each other's antecedents back to the Middle Ages but we have no secrets.

FANNY *(almost in tears).* Everything takes it's toll on Arthur. Just look at his appearance. He's old beyond his years.

GILBERT. His appearance is of little consequence to me. It's his *dis*appearance we could not stand. Now tell me ... what's wrong?

FANNY. That phone call was from his brokers, Cooper, Hall and Company. They've gone bankrupt and Arthur's lost his life's savings. Right now, he's in the orchestra room, praying that his late mother is watching over him.

GILBERT. If it's a question of cash, I have lived considerably *below* my head for the last several years and he can have as *much* as he wants for as *long* as he wants, at no interest whatsoever.

FANNY. Bless you, William.

GILBERT. Please, it's surely the most selfish gesture I've ever made. I have always written for money. Writing out of conviction is for people who have inherited wealth. My bank balance is my sole justification of my life as an author. And without Sullivan, it would not be half as robust. Whatever he needs, he has.

FANNY. I won't say anything until after the reviews of tonight's performance. I hope everything goes ...

GILBERT. A Gilbert without a Sullivan would be worthless. When I tell him a joke, he understands at once. Socially, we are miles apart. He hobnobs with royalty and I prefer to have a drink now and again with the chorus. Intellectually, we're like twins joined at the brain. Carte, Sullivan and I are greater as one than the sum of all of our parts. We will be together forever. *(To the cast.)* On stage for the trio!

(LORD CHANCELLOR, LORDS MOUNTARARAT and TOLLOLER move into position. GILBERT addresses them. SULLIVAN enters during the speech, takes his

place next to MRS. RONALDS, mops his brow with a wet towel.)

GILBERT. The optimum condition in the theatre would be if the audience could hum the tunes as they walked *in.* Failing that, we must fill their ears with such merry music that they'll whistle it all the way home in the carriage instead of arguing with their spouses. This next song is my favorite. If it is not *yours,* I do not wish to know that.

(The actor playing TOLLOLER says something to the other two but it's just a mumble.)

GILBERT. What was that you said, Perkins?

TOLLOLER. Nothing, sir.

GILBERT. That was not nothing, that was *something.* Now, tell us all what you said and you have my solemn promise I'll take no action against you.

TOLLOLER. I ... er ... said that you are the most pompous egotist I have ever met in my life.

GILBERT *(holds back from shouting, softens, begins laughing).* You are ... one hundred percent ... correct. But a large, fully-functioning ego is *good* for a man. It keeps him from brooding over the success of his friends. You may begin.

(MUSIC 17: "FAINT HEART NEVER WON FAIR LADY")

LORD MOUNTARARAT.

IF YOU GO IN,
YOU'RE SURE TO WIN,

YOURS WILL BE THE CHARMING MAIDIE,
BE YOUR LAW,
THE ANCIENT SAW
"FAINT HEART NEVER WON FAIR LADY!"
NEVER, NEVER, NEVER

TRIO.

FAINT HEART NEVER WON FAIR LADY
EVERY JOURNEY HAS AN END.
WHEN AT THE WORST AFFAIRS WILL MEND,
DARK THE DAWN WHEN DAY IS NIGH,
HUSTLE YOUR HORSE AND DON'T SAY DIE!

LORD TOLLOLER.

HE WHO SHIES
AT SUCH A PRIZE
IS NOT WORTH A MARAVEDI.
BE SO KIND
TO BEAR IN MIND
FAINT HEART NEVER WON FAIR LADY!
NEVER, NEVER, NEVER

TRIO.

FAINT HEART NEVER WON FAIR LADY!
WHILE THE SUN SHINES MAKE YOUR WAY,
WHERE A WILL IS, THERE'S A WAY,
BEARD THE LION IN HIS LAIR,
NONE BUT THE BRAVE DESERVE THE FAIR!

LORD CHANCELLOR.

I'LL TAKE HEART
AND MAKE A START
THOUGH I FEAR THE PROSPECT'S SHADY.
MUCH I'D SPEND

TO GAIN MY END.
FAINT HEART NEVER WON FAIR LADY!
NEVER, NEVER, NEVER

TRIO.

FAINT HEART NEVER WON FAIR LADY!
NOTHING VENTURE, NOTHING WIN,
BLOOD IS THICK, BUT WATER'S THIN,
IN FOR A PENNY, IN FOR A POUND,
IT'S LOVE THAT MAKES THE WORLD GO ROUND.

(TRIO dances. Song ends, then blackout. Stage revolves to ... Int. Savoy Theatre—Backstage—September 25, 1884. SULLIVAN sits at a small piano. Stage is empty, clear of people, sets. Barren. GILBERT stands over SULLIVAN. Both are heavier in weight. [NOTE: Could underscore dialogue with Princess Ida *music.])*

SULLIVAN. Are you quite finished with your diatribe?

GILBERT. No ... *SIR* Arthur. Even your knighthood failed to impress the critics when they wrote their reviews of *Princess Ida*. They've been lying in wait for us ever since you knelt before the Queen. If you spent *more* time at the piano and *less* time cavorting with dukes and barons and earls, we'd be much better off. It seems you will go to any lengths to avoid hard labor. And furthermore ...

SULLIVAN *(interrupts)*. Look, I know you've been jealous ...

GILBERT *(interrupts)*. Jealous? Me? There's not a jealous bit of fat on my body. But to knight *you* and omit me is like praising Damon and damning Pythias!

SULLIVAN. The knighthood was *not* for our work *together*. It was for "The Lost Chord" and "Onward Christian Soldiers" and several concert pieces. She said... "for distinguished talents and services to the art of music." She, or should I say *they*, were *not* amused by your lyrics.

GILBERT. And now, *Sir* Arthur Sullivan questions ideas that *Mr.* Arthur Sullivan would not have thought twice about.

SULLIVAN. If you're referring to that inane magic lozenge concept, I have *always* hated it and shall *continue* to hate it into and beyond my grave!

GILBERT. All I ask is that you open your mind to...

SULLIVAN *(rubs his brow)*. Look, I'm tired. Very tired. And if I have any more music left in me, I want it put to good use. *Iolanthe* has been an enormous success and...

GILBERT. And both of us could live comfortably forever on the interest from the money that *Princess Ida* lost! The way D'Oyly Carte spends money on this theatre, we'll be lucky to see any profits at all!

SULLIVAN. I've made a decision.

GILBERT. Good.

SULLIVAN. I'm quitting.

GILBERT. Not good.

SULLIVAN. I find it isn't *fun* anymore. Fanny and I are going to retire, take the sun and visit all the casinos in France. I don't know which will disappear first, my money or my health, but with any luck, I'll run out of both at the same time.

GILBERT. According to our agreement with Carte, if we don't provide him with a show, we are then responsible for his losses.

SULLIVAN. I signed that agreement?

GILBERT. You did.

SULLIVAN. What was I drinking?

GILBERT. As I recall, it was a '72 Dom Perignon.

SULLIVAN. Hmmm. How about a revival?

GILBERT. We're far too young for that. Revivals are for dead authors. Now, tell me the *real* reason you want to quit.

SULLIVAN *(reaches into his pocket, takes out some newspaper cuttings). Princess Ida*...tedious. *Princess Ida*...a clumsy piece of fluff...and on and on.

GILBERT. I read those reviews as well but our critics mistakenly believe that we are ruined by praise and saved by admonishment. Most of them write because they have to say *something*, not because they have something to *say*.

SULLIVAN. Very well...the *real* reason? I am weary of matching my exquisite melodies to your ludicrous sentiments and topsy-turvy situations. The music must have its own sphere, to arise and speak for itself. And I can't write that until you give me a story with a sense of...reality about it.

(CARTE enters, is unseen by the two arguing men.)

GILBERT. Reality? Reality is in the *newspapers*! Reality is war, famine, plague and pestilence. People come to the theatre because it's the only place left where they can *forget* reality. *(Beat.)* I am quite willing to step aside and to even help you find another collaborator.

CARTE. Just a moment, gentlemen. You may be making statements in haste you will regret at leisure.

GILBERT & SULLIVAN *(simultaneously)*. Did we ask for your opinion?

CARTE. No. You never do. But this time you're going to get it! William, you are, by everyone's admission, including your own, a genius. Arthur... I beg your pardon, *Sir* Arthur...

SULLIVAN. Call me Arthur.

CARTE. Arthur, your talent is celebrated wherever English is spoken and music is sung. You each had some mild recognition as soloists but it wasn't until I married the two of you that fortunes were made for all of us. You were *dull* without each other and now you're as much a British landmark as the London Bridge. To end this association now is like clamping the lid on a gold mine.

(Both men stare at D'OYLY CARTE, then at each other for a long, long beat. Finally...)

SULLIVAN *(to GILBERT)*. Do you have... any *other* thoughts beyond that magic lozenge, which shall remain nameless?

GILBERT *(warming to it)*. Well, I must admit I *did* have another concept. It's not quite formed yet but I've come up with several splendid song ideas. It happened the other night as I was pacing the floor in my den. Evidently, I could lose a stone or two and my tread was hardly cat-like. Actually, I walked with such a heavy thump that it dislodged a Japanese sword from my wall which fell on my foot, the one with the gout. I spent the next thirty minutes alternately screaming with pain and smiling with delight as the plot unveiled itself in my mind. It all takes place in the little town of Titipu.

CARTE. Is that near Liverpool?

GILBERT. No, it's in Japan.

SULLIVAN. Japan? What do we know about Japan?

GILBERT. Absolutely nothing! But neither does anyone else! Listen...

(Blackout. Stage revolves to reveal... Int. Savoy Theatre—stage—March 14, 1885—night. Set of the Courtyard of Ko-Ko's Palace in Titipu. Japanese NOBLES discovered standing and sitting in attitudes suggested by native drawings. Full makeup and costumes.)

(MUSIC 18: "IF YOU WANT TO KNOW WHO WE ARE")

CHORUS.

IF YOU WANT TO KNOW WHO WE ARE,
WE ARE GENTLEMEN OF JAPAN.
ON MANY A VASE AND JAR,
ON MANY A SCREEN AND FAN,
WE FIGURE IN LIVELY PAINT.
OUR ATTITUDE'S QUEER AND QUAINT,
YOU'RE WRONG IF YOU THINK IT AIN'T, OH...

IF YOU THINK WE ARE WORKED BY STRINGS
LIKE A JAPANESE MARIONETTE,
YOU DON'T UNDERSTAND THESE THINGS,
IT IS SIMPLY COURT ETIQUETTE.
PERHAPS YOU SUPPOSE THIS THRONG
CAN'T KEEP IT UP ALL DAY LONG?
IF THAT'S YOUR IDEA, YOU'RE WRONG

(NANKI-POO enters, in great excitement. He carries a guitar on his back and a bundle of ballads in his hand.)

(MUSIC 19: "A WANDERING MINSTREL")

NANKI-POO *(spoken).*

GENTLEMEN, I PRAY YOU TELL ME
WHERE A GENTLE MAIDEN DWELLETH
NAMED YUM-YUM, THE WARD OF KO-KO?
IN PITY SPEAK—OH, SPEAK, I PRAY YOU!

NOBLE. Why, who are you to ask this question?

NANKI-POO. Come, gather round me and I'll tell you.
(Sings.)

A WANDERING MINSTREL, I
A THING OF SHREDS AND PATCHES,
OF BALLADS, SONGS AND SNATCHES
AND DREAMY LULLABY.
MY CATALOGUE IS LONG,
THROUGH EVERY PASSION RANGING,
AND TO YOUR HUMORS CHANGING
I TUNE MY SUPPLE SONG.
I TUNE MY SUPPLE SONG.
ARE YOU IN SENTIMENTAL MOOD?
I'LL SIGH WITH YOU.
OH, SORROW,
ON MAIDEN'S COLDNESS DO YOU BROOD?

I'LL DO SO, TOO—
OH, SORROW, SORROW!
I'LL CHARM YOUR WILLING EARS
WITH SONGS OF LOVERS' FEARS
WHILE SYMPATHETIC TEARS
MY CHEEKS BEDEW—
OH, SORROW, SORROW!

BUT IF PATRIOTIC SENTIMENT IS WANTED,
I'VE PATRIOTIC BALLADS CUT AND DRIED,
FOR WHERE'ER OUR COUNTRY'S BANNER MAY BE PLANTED,
ALL OTHER LOCAL BANNERS ARE DEFIED!
OUR WARRIORS, IN SERRIED RINGS ASSEMBLED
NEVER QUAIL—OR THEY CONCEAL IT IF THEY DO,
AND I SHOULDN'T BE SURPRISED IF NATIONS TREMBLED
BEFORE THE MIGHTY TROOPS THE TROOPS OF TITIPU!

CHORUS.

WE SHOULDN'T BE SURPRISED IF NATIONS TREMBLED, TREMBLED
WITH ALARM BEFORE THE MIGHTY TROOPS, THE TROOPS OF TITIPU.

NANKI-POO.

AND IF YOU CALL FOR A SONG OF THE SEA,
WE'LL HEAVE THE CAPSTAN ROUND.
WITH A YO HEAVE HO, FOR THE WIND IS FREE,
HER ANCHOR'S A-TRIP AND HER HELM'S A-LEE,
HURRAH FOR THE HOMEWARD BOUND.

CHORUS.

YO HO—HEAVE HO.
HURRAH FOR THE HOMEWARD BOUND.

NANKI-POO.

TO LAY ALOFT IN A HOWLING BREEZE

MAY TICKLE A LANDSMAN'S TASTE,
BUT THE HAPPIEST HOURS A SAILOR SEES
IS WHEN HE'S DOWN,
AT AN INLAND TOWN,
WITH HIS NANCY ON HIS KNEES, YO-HO!
AND HIS ARM AROUND HER WAIST!

CHORUS.
THEN MAN THE CAPSTAN—OFF WE GO,
AS THE FIDDLER SWINGS US ROUND,
WITH A YO HEAVE HO!
AND A RUM BELOW,
HURRAH FOR THE HOMEWARD BOUND,

(Repeat as indicated in music.)

NANKI-POO.
A WANDERING MINSTREL, I
A THING OF SHREDS AND PATCHES,
OF BALLADS, SONGS AND SNATCHES,
AND DREAMY LULLABY
AND DREAMY LULLABY,
LULLABIES. *(Exits.)*

(MUSIC 20: "DEFER, DEFER" "AS SOMEDAY IT MAY HAPPEN")

CHORUS.
BEHOLD THE LORD HIGH EXECUTIONER!
A PERSONAGE OF NOBLE RANK AND TITLE,
A DIGNIFIED AND POTENT OFFICER,
WHOSE FUNCTIONS ARE PARTICULARLY VITAL!
DEFER, DEFER!

TO THE LORD HIGH EXECUTIONER
DEFER, DEFER,
TO THE NOBLE LORD,
TO THE NOBLE LORD,
TO THE LORD HIGH EXECUTIONER

(KO-KO enters in full regalia.)

KO-KO.

AS SOMEDAY IT MAY HAPPEN
THAT A VICTIM MUST BE FOUND,
I'VE GOT A LITTLE LIST,
I'VE GOT A LITTLE LIST,
OF SOCIETY OFFENDERS
WHO MIGHT WELL BE UNDERGROUND,
AND WHO NEVER WOULD BE MISSED,
WHO NEVER WOULD BE MISSED.
THERE'S THE PESTILENTIAL NUISANCES
WHO WRITE FOR AUTOGRAPHS,
ALL PEOPLE WHO HAVE FLABBY HANDS
AND IRRITATING LAUGHS.
ALL CHILDREN WHO ARE UP ON DATES
AND FLOOR YOU WITH 'EM FLAT.
ALL PERSONS WHO IN SHAKING HANDS,
SHAKE HANDS WITH YOU LIKE *THAT*!
AND ALL THIRD PERSONS WHO
ON SPOILING TETE-A-TETES INSIST,
THEY'D NONE OF THEM BE MISSED,
THEY'D NONE OF THEM BE MISSED

CHORUS.

HE'S GOT 'EM ON THE LIST,
HE'S GOT 'EM ON THE LIST.

AND THEY'LL NONE OF 'EM BE MISSED,
THEY'LL NONE OF 'EM BE MISSED!

KO-KO.

THERE'S THE BANJO SERENADER,
WHOM THE BOURGEOISIE EMBRACE
AND THE PIANO-ORGANIST,
I'VE GOT HIM ON THE LIST.
AND THE PEOPLE WHO EAT PEPPERMINT
AND PUFF IT IN YOUR FACE,
THEY NEVER WOULD BE MISSED,
THEY NEVER WOULD BE MISSED.
THEN THE IDIOT, WHO PRAISES
WITH ENTHUSIASTIC TONE,
ALL CENTURIES BUT THIS,
AND EVERY COUNTRY BUT HIS OWN.

AND THE LADY FROM THE PROVINCES,
WHO DRESSES LIKE A GUY.
AND WHO "DOESN'T THINK SHE DANCES
BUT WOULD RATHER LIKE TO TRY"!
AND THAT SINGULAR ANOMALY,
THE LADY NOVELIST I DON'T THINK
SHE'D BE MISSED.
I'M *SURE* SHE WON'T BE MISSED.

CHORUS.

HE'S GOT HER ON THE LIST,
HE'S GOT HER ON THE LIST.
AND I DON'T THINK SHE'LL BE MISSED,
I'M *SURE* SHE'LL NOT BE MISSED!

KO-KO.

AND THAT NISI PRIUS NUISANCE,

WHO JUST NOW IS RATHER RIFE,
THE JUDICIAL HUMORIST,
I'VE GOT *HIM* ON THE LIST!
ALL FUNNY FELLOWS, COMIC MEN
AND CLOWNS OF PRIVATE LIFE,
THEY'D NONE OF 'EM BE MISSED,
THEY'D NONE OF 'EM BE MISSED.
AND APOLOGETIC STATESMEN
OF THE COMPROMISING KIND,
SUCH AS WHADDYECALLEM—THINGAMABOB
AND LIKEWISE. NEVER MIND.
AND ST-ST-ST AND WHAT'S-HIS-NAME
AND ALSO YOU-KNOW-WHO!
THE TASK OF FILLING IN THESE BLANKS
I'D RATHER LEAVE TO *YOU*.
BUT IT REALLY DOESN'T MATTER
WHOM YOU PUT UPON THE LIST,
FOR THEY'D NONE OF 'EM BE MISSED,
THEY'D NONE OF THEM...
BE MISSED!

CHORUS.

YOU MAY PUT 'EM ON THE LIST,
YOU MAY PUT 'EM ON THE LIST,
AND THEY'LL NONE OF 'EM BE MISSED,
THEY'LL NONE OF 'EM BE MISSED!

(Song ends. MALE CHORUS and KO-KO exit R. FEMALE CHORUS enters led by YUM-YUM, PITTI-SING, PEEP-BO.)

(MUSIC 21: "THREE LITTLE MAIDS")

TRIO.

THREE LITTLE MAIDS FROM SCHOOL ARE WE,
PERT AS A SCHOOL-GIRL WELL CAN BE,
FILLED TO THE BRIM WITH GIRLISH GLEE,
THREE LITTLE MAIDS FROM SCHOOL.

YUM-YUM.

EVERYTHING IS A SOURCE OF FUN!
(Giggle.)

PEEP-BO.

NOBODY'S SAFE, FOR WE CARE FOR NONE!
(Giggle.)

PITTI-SING.

LIFE IS A JOKE THAT HAS JUST BEGUN!
(Giggle.)

TRIO.

THREE LITTLE MAIDS FROM SCHOOL!

CHORUS & TRIO.

THREE LITTLE MAIDS WHO, ALL UNWARY,
COME FROM A LADIES SEMINARY,
FREED FROM ITS GENIUS TUTELARY...

PEEP-BO *(suddenly demure)*.

THREE LITTLE MAIDS FROM SCHOOL!
THREE LITTLE MAIDS FROM SCHOOL!

YUM-YUM.

ONE LITTLE MAID IS A BRIDE, YUM-YUM,

PEEP-BO.

TWO LITTLE MAIDS IN ATTENDANCE COME,

PITTI-SING.

THREE LITTLE MAIDS IS THE TOTAL SUM,

TRIO.

THREE LITTLE MAIDS FROM SCHOOL!

YUM-YUM.

FROM THREE LITTLE MAIDS, TAKE ONE AWAY,

PEEP-BO.

TWO LITTLE MAIDS REMAIN, AND THEY—

PITTI-SING.

WON'T HAVE TO WAIT VERY LONG, THEY SAY...

TRIO.

THREE LITTLE MAIDS FROM SCHOOL!
THREE LITTLE MAIDS FROM SCHOOL!

CHORUS & TRIO *(dancing)*.

THREE LITTLE MAIDS WHO, ALL UNWARY,
COME FROM A LADIES SEMINARY,
FREED FROM ITS GENIUS TUTELARY.

TRIO *(suddenly demure)*.

THREE LITTLE MAIDS FROM SCHOOL!
THREE LITTLE MAIDS FROM SCHOOL!

(Song ends. CHORUS, PITTI-SING, PEEP-BO exit. YUM-YUM stays. NANKI-POO and KO-KO enter.)

YUM-YUM. Darling, I don't want to appear selfish, and I don't suppose I shall ever love anyone else half as much—but when I agreed to marry you—my own—I had no idea, pet, that I should be buried alive in a month.

(NANKI-POO turns to KO-KO who nods sadly.)

KO-KO. By the Mikado's law, when a married man is beheaded, his wife is buried alive.

NANKI-POO. It *does* make a difference, of course.

YUM-YUM. Burial alive—it's such a ... *stuffy* death. You see my difficulty, don't you?

NANKI-POO. Yes, and I see my own. If I insist on marriage, I doom you to a hideous death. If I release you from your promise, you marry Ko-Ko at once!

(MUSIC 22: "HERE'S A HOW-DEE-DO")

YUM-YUM.

HERE'S A HOW-DEE-DO
IF I MARRY YOU,
WHEN YOUR TIME HAS COME TO PERISH,
THEN THE MAIDEN WHOM YOU CHERISH,
MUST BE SLAUGHTERED, TOO.
HERE'S A HOW-DEE-DO!
HERE'S A HOW-DEE-DO!

NANKI-POO.

HERE'S A PRETTY MESS.
IN A MONTH, OR LESS.

I MUST DIE WITHOUT A WEDDING,
LET THE BITTER TEARS I'M SHEDDING,
WITNESS MY DISTRESS.
HERE'S A PRETTY MESS!
HERE'S A PRETTY MESS!

KO-KO.

HERE'S A STATE OF THINGS!
TO HER LIFE SHE CLINGS,
MATRIMONIAL DEVOTION,
DOESN'T SEEM TO SUIT HER NOTION.
BURIAL IT BRINGS!
HERE'S A STATE OF THINGS!
HERE'S A STATE OF THINGS!

YUM-YUM & NANKI-POO	KO-KO
WITH A PASSION THAT'S INTENSE,	**WITH PASSION THAT'S INTENSE**
I WORSHIP AND ADORE	**YOU WORSHIP AND ADORE**
BUT THE LAWS OF COMMON SENSE,	**BUT THE LAWS OF COMMON SENSE**
WE OUGHTN'T TO IGNORE.	**YOU OUGHTN'T TO IGNORE**
IF WHAT HE SAYS IS TRUE,	**IF WHAT I SAY IS TRUE**
'TIS DEATH TO MARRY YOU.	**'TIS DEATH TO MARRY YOU**
HERE'S A PRETTY STATE OF THINGS,	**HERE'S A PRETTY STATE OF THINGS,**
HERE'S A PRETTY HOW-DEE-DO,	**HERE'S A PRETTY HOW-DEE-DO,**
HERE'S A PRETTY STATE OF THINGS.	**HERE'S A PRETTY STATE OF THINGS,**
A PRETTY STATE OF THINGS.	**A PRETTY STATE OF THINGS!**

YUM-YUM.
HERE'S A HOW-DEE-DO.

NANKI-POO.
HERE'S A HOW-DEE-DO.

KO-KO.
HERE'S A HOW-DEE-DO!

YUM-YUM & NANKI-POO.
FOR IF WHAT HE SAYS IS TRUE,
I CANNOT, CANNOT MARRY YOU.
HERE'S A PRETTY, PRETTY
STATE OF THINGS.

TRIO.
HERE'S A PRETTY HOW-DEE-DO!

(Song ends. They exit. Enter procession heralding MIKADO and KATISHA.)

(MUSIC 23: "MIYA SAMA,"
"A MORE HUMANE MIKADO")

CHORUS.
MIYA SAMA, MIYA SAMA
ON N'M-MA NO MAYE NI
PIRA-PIRA SURU NO WA
NAN GIA NA
TOKO TONYARE TONYARE NA?

MIKADO.
FROM EVERY KIND OF MAN

OBEDIENCE I EXPECT.
I'M THE EMPEROR OF JAPAN!

KATISHA.

AND I'M HIS DAUGHTER-IN-LAW ELECT!
HE'LL MARRY HIS SON,
HE'S GOT ONLY ONE,
TO HIS DAUGHTER-IN-LAW ELECT!

MIKADO.

MY MORALS HAVE BEEN DECLARED
PARTICULARLY CORRECT!

KATISHA.

BUT THEY'RE NOTHING AT ALL,
COMPARED WITH THOSE OF HIS
DAUGHTER-IN-LAW ELECT!
BOW, BOW!
TO HIS DAUGHTER-IN-LAW ELECT!

CHORUS.

BOW, BOW!
TO HIS DAUGHTER-IN-LAW ELECT.

MIKADO.

IN A FATHERLY KIND OF WAY,
I GOVERN EACH TRIBE AND SECT.
ALL CHEERFULLY OWN MY SWAY!

KATISHA.

EXCEPT HIS DAUGHTER-IN-LAW ELECT!
AS TOUGH AS A BONE,
WITH A WILL OF HER OWN,
IS HIS DAUGHTER-IN-LAW ELECT!

MIKADO.

MY NATURE IS LOVE AND LIGHT,
MY FREEDOM FROM ALL DEFECT!

KATISHA.

IS INSIGNIFICANT QUITE
COMPARED TO HIS DAUGHTER-IN-LAW ELECT!
BOW, BOW!
TO HIS DAUGHTER-IN-LAW ELECT!

CHORUS.

BOW, BOW!
TO HIS DAUGHTER-IN-LAW ELECT!

MIKADO.

A MORE HUMANE MIKADO
NEVER DID IN JAPAN EXIST!
TO NOBODY SECOND,
I'M CERTAINLY RECKONED,
A TRUE PHILANTHROPIST!
IT IS MY VERY HUMAN ENDEAVOR
TO MAKE, TO SOME EXTENT,
EACH EVIL LIVER, A RUNNING RIVER,
OF HARMLESS MERRIMENT!

MY OBJECT ALL SUBLIME
I SHALL ACHIEVE IN TIME!
TO LET THE PUNISHMENT FIT THE CRIME!
THE PUNISHMENT FIT THE CRIME!
AND MAKE EACH PRISONER PENT
UNWILLINGLY REPRESENT,
A SOURCE OF INNOCENT MERRIMENT,
OF INNOCENT MERRIMENT!

ALL PROSY DULL SOCIETY SINNERS
WHO CHATTER AND BLEAT AND BORE
ARE SENT TO HEAR SERMONS
FROM MYSTICAL GERMANS
WHO PREACH FROM TEN TILL FOUR!

THE AMATEUR TENOR, WHOSE VOCAL
VILLANIES
ALL DESIRE TO SHIRK,
SHALL, DURING OFF-HOURS,
EXHIBIT HIS POWERS
TO MADAME TUSSAUD'S WAXWORK!

THE LADY WHO DYES A CHEMICAL YELLOW,
OR STAINS HER GREY HAIR PUCE,
OR PINCHES HER FIGGER,
IS PAINTED WITH VIGOUR
AND PERMANENT WALNUT JUICE!

THE IDIOT WHO, IN RAILWAY CARRIAGES,
SCRIBBLES ON WINDOW PANES
WE ONLY SUFFER
TO RIDE ON A BUFFER
IN PARLIAMENTARY TRAINS.

MY OBJECT ALL SUBLIME
I SHALL ACHIEVE IN TIME!
TO LET THE PUNISHMENT FIT THE CRIME!
THE PUNISHMENT FIT THE CRIME!
AND MAKE EACH PRISONER PENT,
UNWILLINGLY REPRESENT,
A SOURCE OF INNOCENT MERRIMENT,
OF INNOCENT MERRIMENT!

CHORUS.

HIS OBJECT ALL SUBLIME,
HE WILL ACHIEVE IN TIME!
TO LET THE PUNISHMENT FIT THE CRIME!
THE PUNISHMENT FIT THE CRIME!
AND MAKE EACH PRISONER PENT
UNWILLINGLY REPRESENT,
A SOURCE OF INNOCENT MERRIMENT,
OF INNOCENT MERRIMENT!

MIKADO.

THE ADVERTISING QUACK WHO WEARIES
WITH TALES OF COUNTLESS CURES,
HIS TEETH, I'VE ENACTED
SHALL ALL BE EXTRACTED
BY TERRIFIED AMATEURS.

THE MUSIC HALL SINGER ATTENDS A SERIES
OF MASSES AND FUGUES AND "OPS"
BY BACH, INTERWOVEN
WITH SPOHR AND BEETHOVEN,
AT CLASSICAL MONDAY POPS!

THE BILLIARD SHARP WHOM ANY ONE CATCHES,
HIS DOOM EXTREMELY HARD.
HE'S MADE TO DWELL
IN A DUNGEON CELL
ON A SPOT THAT'S ALWAYS BARRED!

AND THERE HE PLAYS EXTRAVAGANT MATCHES
IN FITLESS FINGER STALLS,
ON A CLOTH UNTRUE,

WITH A TWISTED CUE,
AND ELLIPTICAL BILLIARD BALLS!

MY OBJECT ALL SUBLIME,
I SHALL ACHIEVE IN TIME!
TO LET THE PUNISHMENT FIT THE CRIME!
THE PUNISHMENT FIT THE CRIME!
AND MAKE EACH PRISONER PENT,
UNWILLINGLY REPRESENT,
A SOURCE OF INNOCENT MERRIMENT,
OF INNOCENT MERRIMENT!

CHORUS.

HIS OBJECT ALL SUBLIME,
HE WILL ACHIEVE IN TIME.
TO LET THE PUNISHMENT FIT THE CRIME,
THE PUNISHMENT FIT THE CRIME!
AND MAKE EACH PRISONER PENT,
UNWILLINGLY REPRESENT,
A SOURCE OF INNOCENT MERRIMENT,
OF INNOCENT MERRIMENT!

(Song ends. All exit. YUM-YUM and NANKI-POO enter, holding hands, gazing into each other's eyes. KO-KO runs on, out of breath.)

KO-KO. A terrible thing has happened, Nanki-Poo. It seems you are the son of the Mikado.

NANKI-POO. Yes, but that happened some time ago.

KO-KO. Your Father is here. With Katisha!

NANKI-POO *(to YUM-YUM)*. Katisha claims me in marriage but I can't marry her because I'm now married to you. Consequently, she will insist on my execution, and if I'm executed, my wife will have to be buried alive.

KO-KO. Exactly.

NANKI-POO. But you have supposedly already executed me and if they learn you've lied, it's off with your head.

KO-KO. Gulp.

NANKI-POO. There's one chance. Persuade Katisha to marry you, and she'll have no further claim on me. In that case, I could come to life with no fear of being put to death!

KO-KO. Marry Katisha? Have you *seen* her? She's something appalling.

YUM-YUM. Oh, but that's only her *face*. She has a left elbow people come miles to see.

NANKI-POO. And her right heel is much admired by connoisseurs.

KO-KO. My good sir, I decline to pin my heart upon any lady's right heel.

NANKI-POO. It comes to this, while Katisha is single, I must remain a disembodied spirit. When Katisha is married, existence will be as welcome as the flowers that bloom in the spring.

(MUSIC 24: "THE FLOWERS THAT BLOOM IN THE SPRING")

NANKI-POO.

THE FLOWERS THAT BLOOM IN THE SPRING,
TRA LA
BREATHE PROMISE OF MERRY SUNSHINE.
AS WE MERRILY DANCE AND WE SING,
TRA LA
WE WELCOME THE HOPE THAT THEY BRING,
TRA LA!

OF A SUMMER OF ROSES AND WINE
OF A SUMMER OF ROSES AND WINE.
AND THAT'S WHAT WE MEAN
WHEN WE SAY THAT A THING
IS WELCOME AS FLOWERS
THAT BLOOM IN THE SPRING.
TRA LA LA LA LA LA, ETC. *(Repeat.)*
THE FLOWERS THAT BLOOM IN THE SPRING

TRIO.

TRA LA LA LA LA LA, ETC.

KO-KO.

THE FLOWERS THAT BLOOM IN THE SPRING,
TRA LA!
HAVE NOTHING TO DO WITH THE CASE
I'VE GOT TO TAKE UNDER MY WING,
TRA LA!
A MOST UNATTRACTIVE OLD THING,
TRA LA!
WITH A CARICATURE OF A FACE
WITH A CARICATURE OF A FACE.
AND THAT'S WHAT I MEAN
WHEN I SAY, OR I SING
"OH, BOTHER THE FLOWERS
THAT BLOOM IN THE SPRING"!
TRA LA LA LA LA, ETC.
OH THE FLOWERS THAT BLOOM IN THE SPRING

TRIO.

TRA LA LA LA LA, ETC.

(Song ends. NANKI-POO looks offstage.)

NANKI-POO. Here she comes! You must convince her of your love. Three lives hang in the balance.

(NANKI-POO and YUM-YUM race off. KATISHA enters. Sadly, KO-KO approaches her. Very melodramatic.)

KO-KO. Katisha, for years I have loved you with a white-hot passion whose inner fires are broiling the soul within me.

KATISHA. You! The miscreant who robbed me of my love. You dare to address the woman you have so foully wronged!

KO-KO. Katisha, my fire will not be soothed, it defies all attempts at extinction! I dare not hope for your love, but I will not live without it! Accept my love, or I perish on the spot.

KATISHA. Go! Who knows so well as I that no one ever died of a broken heart!

KO-KO. You know not what you say. Listen...

(MUSIC 25: "TITWILLOW")

KO-KO.

ON A TREE BY A RIVER A LITTLE TOM-TIT
SANG "WILLOW, TITWILLOW, TITWILLOW"
AND I SAID TO HIM "DICKY-BIRD,
WHY DO YOU SIT
SINGING "WILLOW, TITWILLOW,
TITWILLOW?"
"IS IT WEAKNESS OF INTELLECT, BIRDIE?"
I CRIED.
"OR A RATHER TOUGH WORM
IN YOUR LITTLE INSIDE?"
WITH A SHAKE OF HIS POOR LITTLE HEAD

HE REPLIED,
"OH WILLOW, TITWILLOW, TITWILLOW."
HE SLAPPED AT HIS CHEST
AS HE SAT ON THAT BOUGH, SINGING
"WILLOW, TITWILLOW, TITWILLOW"
AND A COLD PERSPIRATION
BESPANGLED HIS BROW
"OH, WILLOW, TITWILLOW, TITWILLOW!"
HE SOBBED AND HE SIGHED,
AND A GURGLE HE GAVE,
THEN HE PLUNGED HIMSELF INTO
THE BILLOWY WAVE,
AND AN ECHO AROSE
FROM THE SUICIDE'S GRAVE,
"OH, WILLOW, TITWILLOW, TITWILLOW."
NOW I FEEL JUST AS SURE
AS I'M SURE THAT MY NAME
ISN'T WILLOW, TITWILLOW, TITWILLOW.
THAT 'TWAS BLIGHTED AFFECTION
THAT MADE HIM EXCLAIM
"OH, WILLOW, TITWILLOW, TITWILLOW."
AND IF YOU REMAIN CALLOUS
AND OBDURATE, I
SHALL PERISH AS HE DID
AND YOU WILL KNOW WHY,
THOUGH I PROBABLY SHALL NOT
EXCLAIM AS I DIE
"OH, WILLOW, TITWILLOW, TITWILLOW"

(Song ends. During above, KATISHA has been greatly affected and is now almost in tears.)

KATISHA. Did he really die of love? All on account of a cruel little hen?

KO-KO. Yes. It's true. I knew the bird intimately. His devotion was something extraordinary.

KATISHA *(still whimpering)*. And if I refuse you, you will go and do the same?

KO-KO. At once.

KATISHA *(falls on his breast)*. You mustn't. Will you continue to love me even though I'm just a teeny-weeny wee bit ... bloodthirsty?

KO-KO. Of course ... There is beauty even in bloodthirstiness.

(The MIKADO enters with his entourage.)

MIKADO. Now then, produce the villain who slayed my heir apparent. The oil is boiling and I've other appointments.

(NANKI-POO and YUM-YUM enter.)

NANKI-POO. The heir apparent is not slain!

MIKADO. Bless my heart. My son!

YUM-YUM. And your daughter-in-law ... elected!

KATISHA *(to KO-KO)*. You have deceived me!

MIKADO. Someone had better explain all this.

(As one, everyone in the cast snaps their heads to look at KO-KO. The MIKADO walks to him, places his huge hands on the man's shoulder.)

KO-KO *(jittery)*. Your Majesty, it's true I stated that I had killed Nanki-Poo but when Your Majesty says "let a thing be done" it's as good as done ... practically, it *is* done, because Your Majesty's word is law. You say "kill someone" and he's as good as dead, practically he is dead! And if he's dead, why not say so?

MIKADO. Hmmm. Yes, I see. Well, nothing could possibly be more satisfactory.

(MUSIC 26: "FINALE")

PITTI-SING.
FOR HE'S GONE AND MARRIED YUM-YUM!

ALL.
YUM-YUM!

PITTI-SING.
YOUR ANGER PRAY BURY,
FOR ALL WILL BE MERRY,
I THINK YOU HAD BETTER SUCCUMB!

ALL.
CUMB-CUMB!

PITTI-SING.
AND JOIN OUR CELEBRATION OF GLEE

KO-KO.
ON THIS SUBJECT I PRAY YOU BE DUMB,

ALL.
DUMB, DUMB!

KO-KO.

YOUR NOTIONS, THOUGH MANY,
ARE NOT WORTH A PENNY,
THE WORD FOR YOUR GUIDANCE IS "MUM"!

ALL.

MUM-MUM!

KO-KO.

YOU'VE A VERY GOOD BARGAIN IN ME!

ALL.

ON THIS SUBJECT WE PRAY YOU BE DUMB,
DUMB-DUMB,
WE THINK YOU HAD BETTER SUCCUMB,
CUMB-CUMB!
YOU'LL FIND THERE ARE MANY,
WHO'LL WED FOR A PENNY, WHO'LL WED FOR A PENNY
THERE ARE LOTS OF GOOD FISH IN THE SEA!

(Repeat as indicated in music.)

YUM-YUM & NANKI-POO.

THE THREATENED CLOUD HAS PASSED AWAY,
AND BRIGHTLY SHINES THE DAWNING DAY.
WHAT THO THE NIGHT
MAY COME TOO SOON,
WE'VE YEARS AND YEARS
OF AFTERNOON!

ALL.

THEN LET THE THRONG,
OUR JOY ADVANCE,
WITH LAUGHING SONG,

AND MERRY DANCE,
WITH LAUGHING SONG
WITH JOYOUS SHOUT,
WITH JOYOUS SHOUT
AND RINGING CHEER,
INAUGURATE THEIR NEW CAREER!

(Repeat twice to finale.)

(Cast freezes in position. Go to black. Stage revolves to ... Int. Rupert D'Oyly Carte's living room. RUPERT is still in his chair, BRIDGET sits at his feet.)

BRIDGET. It sounds as though they all lived happily ever after.

RUPERT. Not quite. They had a horrendous battle about the price of a carpet for the lobby of the Savoy. Gilbert didn't talk to my father or Sullivan for months.

BRIDGET. Did they write anymore?

RUPERT. Oh yes, they finally shook hands and did five more shows, three hits and two misses. Sullivan, whom everyone reckoned to be a hypochondriac, died at 58, probably saying "You see? I *was* sick." My father, whom we believed had the constitution of a Cossack, was gone at the age of 57. And now, Gilbert. But their work lives on. *(Beat.)* And if I have *my* way, it will live on forever.

(RUPERT and BRIDGET exit. Stage revolves to ... Cast, still in position, sings REPRISE 26 (A) and bows are taken.)

CURTAIN

DIRECTOR'S NOTES

DIRECTOR'S NOTES

DIRECTOR'S NOTES

DIRECTOR'S NOTES